REBEL MILLIONAIRE

KATRINA RUTH

WORLDCHANGERS
M E D I A

Hardcover: 978-1-955811-14-9
Paperback: 978-1-955811-10-1
Ebook: 978-1-955811-11-8
LCCN: 2021925252

First hardcover edition: September 2022

Edited by Bryna Haynes/www.WorldChangers.media
Cover design by WorldChangers Media
Photography: Kit Wise/Wise Photography
Layout by Paul Baillie-Lane/www.pblpublishing.co.uk

Published by WorldChangers Media
PO Box 83, Foster, RI 02825
www.WorldChangers.Media

DEDICATION

To the ones who have always known they were born for more, and are ready to motherfucking claim it.

Your time is now.

It always was.

CONTENTS

Introduction   1

Chapter 1: Born For More   13

Chapter 2: It Was Always in You   33

Chapter 3: You Don't Need Permission   55

Chapter 4: Desire   77

Chapter 5: What Do You Care About?   111

Chapter 6: You Were Made This Way   135

Chapter 7: Playing in the Quantum   155

Chapter 8: You Are the Niche   181

Chapter 9: The Money Switch, Bitch   207

Chapter 10: The Rebel Life   235

Acknowledgments   246

Resources   248

About the Author   249

About the Publisher   250

INTRODUCTION

Imagine standing in a big, open room. You believe this room to be the entire world. *Your* world.

As you look around, you notice that everything in this room—your business, relationships, lifestyle, money, and art—is everything you've ever known. And you wonder, "Is this really my life? Is this everything? Is this windowless room *all there is?*"

You continue to look under every chair and in every corner, yet you can't seem to find anything that truly excites your spirit.

Then, just for fun, you begin to imagine what this space would look like if it were clear, expanded, open ... new. You feel a desire bubbling up inside of you—a desire to unleash everything you've been holding back, everything you categorized as *too much, out of reach, over the top.*

You ask yourself, "How can I bring my dreams to life? What else is possible for me?"

And then, finally, "What is beyond these walls?"

Suddenly, for some reason known only to God (and your deepest self), you push right up against one wall of that room—the edge of the world as you know it!—

And it falls away.

You fall through.

You spiral down like Alice through the looking glass, and you see, for the first time, another world—a world that part of you always knew existed, but that you never had a name for. And as you float down gently (or land with a bone-crunching crash, whichever way you imagine it), you realize that you have no idea what to do in this place. You have no idea who to be, or how. It's terrifying.

Who are you? What is life about? What are the rules, and how does it all work?

What do you do now?

What you don't yet realize—because it doesn't exist in the paradigm of the room you just left—is that you are suddenly, fully, *becoming*. And as you become, you are also deeply remembering who you always have been.

In that moment of remembrance, a switch gets flicked.

The switch.

Suddenly, every last bit of "should" and "has to" and "that's the way it just is" falls away. The room you thought was the entire world, your only world, was revealed as an illusion, and you broke free.

Part of you sees that everything you have ever wanted is possible. That there is more to life than you ever imagined, and that, in this new expanse on the other side of conformity, you are free to claim it all.

Part of you wants to run, screaming, back to the safety of the room you once knew. "Maybe," this part whispers, "you're making things up." Maybe you're a bad person for asking for more.

The thing is, once you've seen what's beyond the room, you can't unsee it.

You can no longer live your life in that little space, no matter how amazing and wonderful (in some ways) you used to think it was.

And here is what else ...

You fell through the walls of your old paradigm because your soul whispered, "Let go. Listen. Say yes."

You came here to do more than fill in the blanks and connect the dots with other dot-connectors in the tiny, windowless cage that everyone else seems to think is life.

You came here to fully express the glorious, messy, raw, wild, crazy, "what the fuck *is* that?" thing living inside of you. The thing that's killing you softly as you refuse to let it out.

You realise you came here to be a soul who plays beyond the walls.

You came here to be a Rebel.

A Rebel *Millionaire.*

YOUR PERMISSION SLIP

"You're so brave! If you could find a way to bottle and sell 'how to get over your fears,' you'd be rich."

I smiled to myself as I listened to this exchange between a good friend of mine and a friend of hers whom I didn't really know. There was a pause, and then my friend looked at me and laughed.

"That's exactly what Kat does!" she said.

"Pretty much," I returned. In my head, I added, *And I'm also rich. So yeah, that's good stuff to bottle.*

It was one of those moments where you kind of pause in fascination at yourself. Not in an egotistical way, but in a "Holy shit, I can't believe I actually do that!" kind of way. Someone marvels at what you do, and suddenly, you see yourself from outside yourself. You see the whole picture.

I mean ... I may bottle and sell "get over your fears," but I still deal with those fears all the time. I just don't let them rule me anymore.

I explained to the new friend that entrepreneurs get stuck for one of two reasons. Either they think the thing they want is too stupid, too silly, too immature, or too unclear—that it needs to be more "proper" before they put it out there—or they think they need permission from some mystical, official being to live the life they dream of, and be all of who they are.

"No one needs permission," I told her. "We were born with permission. How can you not have permission to be who you really are—the way you see yourself as being, the way you are shown, inside of you? That permission slip was granted before you even came to this Earth. Laminated and certified. What we do have to do, though, is claim it. Decide that it gets to be that simple. And then act from that place inside of us, to bring it to life. No filter. No edits. Just owning it.

"And as for that thing you're thinking of doing?" I continued. "The one you're questioning yourself around? It's right because that is how you see it. 'Proper' is largely about meeting other people's needs for how to live, operate, do business—heck, even breathe! What if the 'proper' thing was to follow the permission slip you were already born with?"

"Wow!" my new friend said. "That's it! I've been waiting for permission!" She paused. I could practically see the truth sinking in.

Then, she asked, "How did you learn to do this?"

Looking back, it seems so clear. The moment I gave myself permission to be all of who I am was the moment my true soul business was born—and also the moment shit really blew up.

I look back now and see so clearly how I'd been blocking the way for myself without even realizing it—how I'd been failing to give myself permission to just go all in on what was inside of me. I'd been doing business for years prior to this shift. But when I truly said yes to what I knew my life was meant to be about—when I decided to give my life fully to what my life was given to me for—my mission expanded. Within months, I started achieving dreams I'd been holding onto for years.

I just kept saying yes. Again, and again, and again.

And the times when I let fear take charge? Everything stopped working, slowed down, or dropped me back into that heavy "stuckness."

I realised it was simple. So much simpler than what I'd been telling myself. Success always is, I've since learned.

But that doesn't necessarily mean it is easy ...

THE ONLY "FORMULA" IS TO BE YOU

There are approximately 580,000,000 entrepreneurs in the world. Most of them are doing it wrong.

Doing *them* wrong, is what I mean.

The world—particularly the online space—is full of people trying to *achieve*. They hustle, but without the flow bit. They grind, but only according to how they've been told. They push, and push, and push some more without checking in to determine if the push is *purposeful*. Aligned. Expansive-making.

Then, once they make some money or some headway, they think they've found the secret. "Just follow my 5-step success formula," they say, "and I'll show you how to make millions. Get famous. Be happy. Be enough. Be *free!*"

And so, like good little room-dwellers, we do what we're told. We execute the strategies. We connect the dots. We follow the 5-step fucking formulas. We do it someone else's way—and snap! It works!

Only ... it doesn't. Not really. Maybe not at all. Because even if some sort of "result" is attained ... so what? It doesn't *mean* anything to us. It's a house of cards we don't even want to keep standing.

The truth is, you didn't come here simply to achieve. You didn't come here to make money and then retire to some cookie-cutter community and do nothing with your gifts for the next however-many-more decades. You didn't come here just to build a business, or even a brand.

You came here to build a *life*.

A life of purpose and calling.

A life of creativity, and freedom, and fulfillment.

A life where you can actually fulfill your destiny.

The moment you start thinking that your mission in life is to get shit done, pay your bills, create something "nice," and maybe someday get to where you can live the VIP life ...

In that moment, you have forgotten who you are, and what this life was always meant to be about.

This book is the break-out-of-the-box playbook for the *driven* ones who know they were born for more—people like *you*, who know, deep down, that they were never meant to live a "normal" life. The leaders, the revolutionaries, the way-makers, the game-changers. The ready-to-go-all-in badasses who know it's time to flip that switch and never, *ever* go back.

You were drawn to this book because you are *done* being a good little Stepfordpreneur. You're done following the rules, making everything Instagram-pretty, and worrying endlessly about whether you're being "proper" or professional enough. Bleugh! You're done journaling and dreaming about the life you someday want, and the freedom you'll someday have, without ever actually pressing play. You're ready to finally show the fuck up, go all in, and be who you came here to be.

The world doesn't need more Stepfordpreneurs. We don't need more people trying to get rich by becoming a pale shadow of someone else who got rich without doing it directly from purpose and soul. We don't need more people falling for the line of, "Do what I say. Build it like this. I can show you the way—just leave your soul at the door over there." I've fallen for that one; maybe you have, too. But now, you've seen beyond the walls, and you're ready—for *real* this time.

FOLLOWING WHAT'S IN YOU WORKS. PERIOD

Since I started my online business (which was somewhere between 2006 and 2010 depending on what you mean by "started," since it was just a blog to support my brick-and-mortar business at first), I've personally received over $20,000,000. I answered my soul's calling gradually, bit by bit, and then eventually with a big, resounding "Fuck, yes!" Along the way, I've taught tens of thousands of students and clients to do the same through the hundreds (yes, literally) of digital courses, classes, programs, workshops, and events I have created and led, as well as through private mentoring for those who want to go all in with me.

The path to becoming a Rebel Millionaire—what I am here to show you, or more accurately to lead you back to, since it's already within you—isn't another "Do as I do and get rich quick, I promise!" formula. It's not another "bro marketing" tactic. In fact, it's not technically marketing at all. I was making millions online before I even heard the words "internet marketing." What I have done to build all this, and what you're about to learn, has nothing in common with those strategies, rules, or "shoulds." In truth, becoming a Rebel Millionaire isn't even *about* making money or building a business—at least, not as a primary focus. It's more about becoming who you were always meant to be, and letting the business and the money that matches that show up.

As for what I teach, well ...

I don't teach people to do what I do, or how to show up like I show up, because that would be impossible. Instead, I take you to the place of being *all* of who you are, and activating that soul remembrance, baby! Along the way, we'll find the stuff you need to do, and how you're gonna do it. (After all, I've been throwing shit at the internet and monetizing the fuck out of it for years, so I know a thing or two about what stuff works.)

But what I really do is help you flick that switch so that what has always been meant to be ...

Is.

This work is all about falling through the walls, landing in your truth, becoming *all* of who you have always been—that fully expressed, wild, messy, free, "Fuck, yes!" you—and at the same time, making killer money and changing the world! In other words, the way it was always gonna be for you!

If you're looking for "Three Simple Steps to Becoming the Next Rebel Millionaire," this is definitely *not* the book for you. But if you're an online entrepreneur, coach, healer, artist, or creative who is sick to death of trying to "hustle" your way to success inside the box, this book is the medicine you need to stop that train for good.

This is the real deal. As raw as it gets.

This is about opening the door to your soul, setting free the screaming joy/art/madness/ message that's inside of you, and actually *becoming* the thing that you've been trying to create for so damn long.

I don't think I have to tell you ...

This work is not for the timid or the faint of heart.

It's for those who are *absolutely unwilling* to die with everything that matters still trapped inside of them.

The ones who were born for more.

The ones who were *never* gonna live the "normal" life.

The *true* Rebel Millionaires.

You.

So, what are you waiting for?

Life is Now. Press Play.

KAT

CHAPTER 1

BORN FOR MORE

In my twenties, I was somehow under the impression that my dream life would just magically *happen* to me. By the time I reached the ripe old age of thirty, surely God Himself would roll up to my door holding a silver platter and say, "Here's that dream life you asked for, Kat!"

Okay, I didn't *actually* think this—or, at least, I wouldn't have said so if you'd asked. But somewhere beneath the surface, I vaguely imagined that, "It's just going to happen, because it's *meant* to."

And, really, by the time I was twenty-six, it must have looked to the outside world like God had delivered. I was a wildly successful personal trainer and fitness expert, married to my business partner, my first husband. People referred to us as the "Ken and Barbie" of our hometown Melbourne's fitness scene. We made great money and lived a luxury lifestyle. We were in fantastic shape. We had the perfect apartment in the perfect part of town, with the perfect car, the perfect clothes, the perfect ... well, fucking *everything*.

And then, my husband started to talk about having a baby.

He wasn't suggesting that we hop to it right away, but he was talking about a family as something that *would be*. And why not? We had everything we could possibly want. This would only be the icing on the cake.

I wanted kids, too, one day. But I was only twenty-six! This conversation, and the recognition of everything that would come with this life he was describing ... It froze me. I couldn't see it. I couldn't feel it. I didn't want it.

Yes, we were living the dream. But it all came to a stop when I realised ...

It was *someone else's* dream.

I remember being shocked—*shocked*—at this truth. I just stood there in numb, silent horror as I realized that I could *die* without ever bringing anything within me to life. That just because I *had* a destiny wasn't a guarantee that I would live it.

In that moment, I knew something had to change.

I had to change.

What followed was an eighteen-month meltdown that I now bemusedly refer to as my "quarter-life crisis." The implosion was swift, dramatic, and messy as all-get-out, and resulted in me high-tailing it out of my perfect "Barbie" lifestyle with only one plate, one knife, one fork, all my books, and my cat, Arnie. I guess I thought that, wherever I was going, it would just be me and the cat.

My husband said to me, as it was all going down, "I should have paid more attention to the titles of your books." They were all about finding happiness, finding your purpose, and living your best life. Maybe he should have. But maybe it was more than that. Maybe the path of finding true soul alignment and becoming who you are meant to be isn't linear or clean-cut.

Those books are still with me, by the way, and are currently scattered all over my home, as books should be. I have no idea what happened to that single plate and its companion cutlery, but Arnie is still alive and well, living his best life with my parents in Melbourne. So maybe everything did end up exactly as it was meant to be!

But back then, oh boy. By the time those eighteen months were over, I was no longer married. I no longer had the perfect apartment, the perfect car, or the perfect savings account. I no longer had any idea who I was, or what the fuck I was doing. The girl I had been, before it all hit the heavens? I had no idea where she'd gone, or even where she'd come from in the first place.

It was a devastating period. I felt deeply lost, forlorn, and so very, very far from purpose. Months went by where I didn't speak to anybody. I hid from my friends and family. I moved through my days like a zombie. There's a photo from that Christmas where I look so vacant and empty, my eyes just gazing hopelessly away into nothing, that it makes me tear up every time I see it.

After all of that upheaval, I was still no closer to my dream life ... but at least I wasn't in the *wrong* life anymore. Deep within me—despite all my questioning and wondering if I had just destroyed my life and everything in it for nothing—I did know that this was the right thing to do.

See, for so long, I didn't have the guts or the know-how (okay, really just the guts) to pull the emergency cord and stop this train that was hurtling me at out-of-control speed into the wrong life. I didn't trust my feelings. I mean, what did I have to complain about? What the hell was wrong with me? But all I could feel was that life—the life I'd fallen into—was forcing me to continue being a person I knew I wasn't, and I didn't know how to change it.

I used to read and journal and think endlessly about what I really wanted—about that life I wanted God to deliver on a silver platter—but then I would get on with my day and go about the business of *not being me.* I hadn't yet realised that I could just flick the switch to be who I was meant to be—who I wanted to be—now!

In so many ways, I was stuck in an old, uncomfortable paradigm of "success." I climbed the ladder within the fitness world. I played the game of competition with people I didn't deeply respect or aspire to be like. I drank and partied 'til all hours because those behaviours were expected of me, not because they felt right. I ignored the signs from God about how my day should flow, and kept my feet on that hamster wheel, because ... well, what else could I do? I bought what I "should" buy, ate what I "should" eat.

I kept my mouth shut when I wanted to scream.

With every day that passed where I didn't own my truth, that speeding train got faster and more dangerous. So it makes sense that, when I finally pulled that cord and jumped off, the collateral damage was ... well, it was fucking huge. I yanked that cord as hard as I could and nearly blew up the whole damned train and everyone in it.

I wish I had been brave enough to pull that cord sooner. If I'd known how much mess I was about to create, I might have done things differently! But the truth is, we always learn and grow through things as we *need* to, so we can learn the lessons our soul is asking to learn. And the fact remains, it was the right thing to do, even with all the (very messy) fallout. Because, what was the alternative? Keep wishing and waiting for God to show up on my doorstep while I slowly suffocated—or wait for life to finally blow up in my face? That train was going down whether I pulled the cord or not. My only choice was whether I was going to let it take me down with it.

That's the thing about life. It's all *for me.*

Just like it's all *for you.*

Not the fake, "perfect" version of you. The *real* you. The oddball. The unicorn. The disruptor. The changemaker.

The Rebel Millionaire.

STOP THE TRAIN

Here's the thing that no one ever tells you.

You came to this crazy, wonderful, chaotic, amazing planet for no other reason than to be *you*. Fully, unapologetically you.

Not to be a meek and mild version of you. Not to be "a little bit" you. Not to be a pale shadow of someone else who "does it better." Not to be the you who is, as one very conformist literary agent once put it to me, "You, Kat, just ... not like that." Not to hop on a train to an "acceptable" life with a bunch of other people who are also accepting their own not-enoughness rather than owning what's inside of them (or who, worse still, haven't thought about it one way or the other.)

Chances are, you're reading this book because you want something different for your life. You read the title, *Rebel Millionaire*, and your soul knew, *That's who I am!*

You know you were born for more than what you're currently living. You know you are different—that you've always *been* different, even from the other entrepreneurs and creatives around you. You know that something powerful is coiled up inside you, and that you can barely breathe because you're trying to keep it locked inside instead of unleashing it into the world.

If you've ever been told stuff like ...

- "You're too intense."

- "You're too much."

- "You're too demanding."

- "You can't have that."

- "You don't fit in."

- "You're doing it wrong."

... if you get the side-eye when you walk into the room, because people can't *not* look at you but they're furious that you're sucking up all the attention ...

... or, alternatively, if you find yourself changing or toning down the way you dress, the way you speak, the way some part of you wants to show up like you own the fucking place ...

You are not broken.

You are a Rebel Millionaire.

The truth is, *you don't have it in you* to be like the others. *You don't have it in you* to follow any pathway except the one your soul is calling you to find, bit by bit. You are different.

You've probably tried for years, even decades, to "do it right"—to be the good girl, to meet the expectations, to be a "proper" woman or wife or employee or entrepreneur. But in the end, you know that nobody else, no matter how amazing they are, understands better than you how to live your life. You always knew that you *must* give in to who you are, fully, truly, and without exception.

But if you really want to live the dream, you have to be willing to pull that emergency cord first. Wherever your life is hurtling toward, if it's not truly aligned with who you are, you need to grit your teeth, square your shoulders (boobs out!) and be honest and brave and committed enough to *stop the damn train*. Now.

You heard me.

Pull. The. Cord.

Because here is the smack-in-the-face, back-to-soul wake-up call you need: You can't get away with living the wrong life forever. In fact, *you have no more time left to live the wrong life.*

Your soul wants *so badly* for you to express yourself and serve other humans in the way you were born to do. If you, in your human form, can't (or won't) summon up the courage to walk away from whatever doesn't feel *that* aligned, your higher self is going to sort that shit out for you outside of your conscious choice—and you're probably not going to like how that goes down when it happens. Life has a way of taking care of business for you if you don't do it yourself.

Sometimes, speeding down the wrong path shows up in big and obvious ways. It could be your relationship. Your entire business model (or even your whole industry). The continent or country where you're living. That

"YOU CAME TO THIS CRAZY, WONDERFUL, CHAOTIC, AMAZING PLANET FOR NO OTHER REASON THAN TO BE YOU."

project or job or relationship you're giving huge chunks of your energy to.

But it could be the less obvious stuff as well. The way you're marketing. That stupid diet you're on. The things you think you "have to" do as a parent. The habits you indulge in your downtime. The hobbies and tasks and to-do's that you think make you a better person, but that don't remotely light you up the way *anything* (or anyone!) you say yes to actually should do.

If the things you do every day don't feel like a full-body *"Fuck, yes!"*, stop giving your life for them. Get real about the fact that, if you were being fully *you*, not only would you not be *doing* this stuff, you wouldn't have noticed or even thought of it!

Gorgeous, I want you to hear me.

The thing about continuing to give your life to the wrong things ...

Is that, by definition, you aren't giving your life to the *right* things.

And if you keep that up, you will die without expressing all that beauty, joy, fierceness, love, passion, and raw badassery that is clawing away at your insides, eating you alive. That outcome would be tragic—and, at the same time, completely ordinary. Just because you were born with a destiny doesn't mean you will ever live it.

What? You think you were the first person on the planet to be born with this sort of inner light? No. We are everywhere. But while many *say* they are rebels, most never fully act on it.

You become the Rebel Millionaire, not when you have cash in your accounts, or designer clothes on your ass, but when you quit letting your bullshit be bigger than your dreams. You know that, when your soul is freed, you will impact millions, make millions, and change the world—all while dancing madly in circles wearing six-inch stilettos, and before the rest of the world has even had breakfast! (Or, you know, whatever your version of that is.)

But knowing isn't the same as doing.

So if you aren't ready to question—

If you aren't ready to see beyond what your eyes allow—

If you feel safe and happy being told how to be, what to strive for, or what success "must" look like—

If you don't hear the call—

Put down this book and walk away. Keep that light tucked away safely inside you. Stay on that speeding train to nowhere.

On the other hand, if you're ready to dial up the volume and step into the "too much," the "over-the-top," the "fuck, yes!" of your life ...

Get ready. Because things are about to get crazy.

STOP WAITING TO BE REAL

I never realized until I blew up my whole world that my "perfect life" vision—you know, the one I thought was so far away and hard to achieve—was all about being *me.*

I spent years telling myself that one day I would do the damn thing, become the damn thing, and finally create all of what I dreamed of and saw. One day, I would make a lot of money—way more than most people ever dreamed of—and do all the stuff I wanted to do. One day, I'd create a lifestyle where I could roll out of bed and just be me, *all day long.* One day, I'd finally figure out how to be the leader, messenger, writer, speaker, and coach I knew I was destined to become.

I knew, deep in my soul, that I was born for more.

And one day, I told myself, it would all just ... come together. One day God would show up with that silver platter!

(Just not *today.* I was busy today. I had too much to do. I didn't know where to start. I wasn't ready!)

Until I pulled that cord, every day was "not today."

That inner voice kept screaming, "You're not good enough! You have *no fucking idea* what you're doing! You're not even a proper adult! You don't even know how to do your hair!" And I kept listening.

What I didn't know was that *every person* who we think has their shit together (or is super talented, or possesses some kind of superhuman discipline) has that same voice screaming in their head. That same voice telling them that they can't do it, that they're not good enough, that their fears are valid, that they shouldn't even try. That voice that says, "Everybody else is smarter, funnier, and has shinier hair than you as well, so don't even bother."

I've mentored hundreds of the world's most amazing leaders, entrepreneurs, creatives, and coaches, and worked with thousands more through my programs and challenges—and I can promise you, self-doubt will *always* try to bite us in the ass and keep us from rising to that next level. It never goes away. You'd be shocked if you could hear the conversations I've had with well-known entrepreneurs, coaches, and creatives—people who *know* that they can't get away with being anything other than who they really are.

The only difference between those who are doing the damn thing and those who are still talking about it is that the people who are doing it ... did it. They recognized that they had the ability to act from self-belief *right now* rather than having to work toward it. They shut the door on fear and said, "Thanks, but this is more important."

Have you done that for *you*?

Are you willing to?

Or are you still waiting for permission?

"

THE THING ABOUT
CONTINUING TO GIVE YOUR
LIFE TO THE *WRONG THINGS*
IS THAT, BY DEFINITION,
YOU AREN'T GIVING YOUR
LIFE TO THE *RIGHT THINGS*.

"

Your dream life will never happen until you consciously decide to *make* it happen. To get out of your own way and commit to being *all* of who you came here to be.

I'll be sharing a lot more of my story in the chapters to come. But for now, know this: I didn't become some sort of superhuman success story overnight. I didn't relentlessly do all the things at once. I sure as hell didn't follow someone else's "proven formula."

I *decided.* And then did the work. The messy, raw, all-over-the-place, chaotic AF *work.* The real work of, bit by bit, following what was inside of me, even (especially) when it made no sense, and I had no idea how to do what was being asked of me.

I worked my ass off to become Katrina Ruth, the version of me you see online. Sure, there are parts you don't see as much. Katrina the mother, daughter, sister, friend, and wife is a lot quieter. She's super introverted, and always has been. She largely wants to be left alone to write, work out, and spend time with her kids and the small bubble of people she calls family and friends. She questions herself ... a lot. She has insecurities, doubts, and fears. Plenty of 'em.

She's human.

Shocking, I know.

But I have another side to me. Katrina Ruth—the show, the personality, the brand? She's me, too. All my life, she's been burning away inside of me, screaming at the top of her lungs, waiting to break out and tear shit up. She is the rebel leader who has created multiple eight figures in soul-aligned income by *just being her*—and she wants to inspire, motivate, empower, and (lovingly) kick your ass so you can do the same.

The quiet Katrina and the fierce Kat are both me. They're both fully authentic. One is my "comfort" state. The other I built, little by little, by following my soul's blueprint. I hustled, celebrated, cried, and raged ... but I never stopped, because I knew this thing coming to life inside me was bigger than who I was being, and the world needed her.

I saw who I was meant to become. And I said yes to her without any proof that it would work—except the only proof that mattered: that I could dare to do such a thing.

And then, I trained myself to *become* her.

(Are you imagining this becoming for yourself? I hope so!)

I repeatedly went against what felt normal, comfortable, and natural at the time. Instead, I chose what felt confronting, reckless, mad, or straight-up impossible. I looked continually into the future, and asked myself, "What is the move I *must* make?"

That commitment got me through the days when I had no money for groceries. The days when I was so scared I wanted to vomit. The days when it would have been easier to do *anything* except this thing I knew I was born to do.

But despite all the challenges, I wake up every single day, and I get to be *me*.

Newsflash: You have one life to live. It's *this one, right here.* This is not a dress rehearsal. Which means it's time to face the reality that *everything you feel inside you is real* and that it's available, specifically to you, right now. You *can* fulfill the destiny you know is calling to you—but if you want it, you have to be willing to do what it takes, no matter what it takes, until it takes, *and then keep going.*

In this book, I'm going to show you how to walk that path—the path of the Rebel Millionaire.

The road forward will probably look a lot different than you expected. I'm not going to bury you in business strategies or tell you how to "follow my proven system." (I'm not you, and you're not me, so you certainly won't be doing it my way!) Instead, I'll show you how to find *your* way to live, work, and lead completely on your own terms, in full accordance with all the magic simmering away inside you.

This isn't about "getting away with" being fully, unapologetically you. This is about recognizing that being fully you is *the only real responsibility you have in this life,* and that it's irresponsible to the entire planet when you say, "Not today."

Yeah, you're in for a wild ride. But don't let that scare you.

You were born for this.

CHAPTER 2

IT WAS ALWAYS IN YOU

When I was eight or so, I found myself standing in one of those endless schoolyard queues. Perhaps we were waiting for a special assembly, or a school concert; I don't remember.

Shuffling my feet in boredom, I glanced up at the girl standing just ahead of me. I didn't know her, but she was maybe a year older than me. She seemed so sad and lost. She had that whole "I don't know how to *be*" vibe going on.

And I thought, *I can help you. I can show you the way.*

The way to confidence. To certainty. To standing tall and upright and proud, and owning who you are.

I can show you the way.

The essence of that thought was so strong that I can still feel it in my body today. It was more than a knowing. It was a certainty—a *soul* certainty.

What's funny is that, at that point in my life, I was the *worst possible example* of confidence, certainty, and owning who I was!

I was always shy growing up. Introverted as fuck.

Gangly. Awkward. It was a total "baby deer learning to walk" situation until I was *at least* eighteen. I was so uncool it almost beggers belief.

Not only did I always have the "wrong" clothes and mannerisms, I was a total dork and always got picked last for team sports. For a good chunk of my primary school years, I spent the daily play break in a tunnelled-out section of bushes on the side of the quadrangle, hidden away with a book. I read so much I maxed out the local library's twenty-book-a-week limit (and sometimes the limits of my siblings and friends, too).

Actually, that's not so far from where I am now. When I'm not jumping around on camera or on a stage, I'm still tucked away somewhere with a book. My favourite place to be is alone with my imagination, my dreams, my words. But back then, I always felt like I was "doing it wrong"—with "it" being whatever the cool kids were doing.

Even my lunches were uncool! I brought brown wholegrain sandwiches long before anyone else was eating them. Sometimes, they were bizarre concoctions like peanut butter and alfalfa with sultanas (and maybe some bananas mashed in).

You can't make this shit up. The upset to the psyche is real!

And yet, that day, something in me looked at that sad, lost girl who was standing there all alone with no clue how to be who she was ... and I just *knew*.

I can help you understand who you are.
I can help you understand how life works.
I can help you find your way.

As I got older, my fascination with understanding people only became stronger. I spent the fifth grade studying psychology and body language. All my school presentations were on these topics. I was already learning to read and understand people—to see beneath the surface, and understand in a heartbeat who they were, what they were hiding from, what they were meant to be living for, and what their soul was fighting and screaming and practically dying for.

What I didn't yet understand was how to do this for *me*.

I was still in that stage of "get me the fuck outta here!" I was still hiding with my books. I was still gangly and uncertain and trying to play this life by the rules. It never occurred to me that this strange *thing* inside of me—this thing telling me to look at life differently, to see beneath the surface—was the gateway to everything I would someday create.

And so, I got the grades. I went to university with the intention of studying law—and then quit straight away because, as it turns out, there is no magic to be found in being told what to do, how to think, or how to function inside other people's processes and systems.

Why would I need that? How was there even a pre-defined "game of life" to have rules and laws *for*?

Obviously (to me, if not to anyone else in my world), this wasn't going to work out.

After that, I turned my focus to my other childhood dream: writing. I decided that I would become a journalist—one held in great esteem, writing for the greatest paper in my home city of Melbourne.

I lasted maybe five weeks on that track. I didn't like being told how to write.

I still hadn't figured myself out. And so, my perspective became that I—the A-plus, top-of-her-class student who was most suited (according to my teachers) for tertiary education and a life to inspire reverence amongst my peers—was *failing horribly.*

What the hell had been the point of it all? I'd spend my whole life becoming the *best* so that I could have the *best* career, and the *best* life, but now all of those "proper" adult pathways just ... repelled me.

Who *was* I?

What was to become of me?

I didn't know. But I couldn't go on as I had been.

I was too scared to tell my parents that I had dropped out of university, so I kept going there every day. I set up a business giving facials in the retail section of campus, using my organic skin care from home and facecloths from Big W. I certainly wasn't qualified to give facials, but it was better than sitting in class.

"

IT'S IMPOSSIBLE FOR
SOMETHING UNIQUE TO
ALSO BE 'NORMAL.'

"

After I finally broke the news to my parents, I went to Europe for a few months. Whilst there, I gained some weight, which I didn't like, so when I got home I became a gym junkie. Then, as a follow-on from that, I became a personal trainer, and ended up spending the next thirteen years in that space—because, hey, why not? At least, that's where the idea began.

I'd never aspired to work in fitness, but I loved it, and working for myself with the support of a large health club allowed me to tap a talent I'd always known I possessed, yet never had quite this sort of opportunity with: sales.

I crushed it. And not just because I was a great trainer.

Within fifteen minutes of meeting me, new clients would go from chatting up their fitness goals to bawling in the members' lounge about the state of their lives and how *not* on purpose they were. They had no idea what had just hit them.

"I thought I was coming here to work out!" they'd wail.

"Yeah, we'll get to that," I'd say. "But there's no point in working out until you know what you want from your life and who you're meant to be. Connect to that, and you won't need willpower—for fitness or anything else."

Most of them were grateful. Some got super pissed off with me, since in mere minutes I'd managed to pull up the truth about what they'd been running from and who they were not being. Over the years, many of my high-level clients quit their corporate and professional careers—lawyers, analysts, CEOs, even a brain surgeon. They would always pop back around and tell me something like, "This is because of the conversations I've had with you. You made me realize what life is about, and I couldn't keep going down the wrong path."

Even today, I can remember the feeling those words gave me. Knowing I'd impacted somebody to live the life they were actually here to live was incredible. Although, honestly, I was a little scared the day the brain surgeon hit me with the news that he was abandoning his chosen career. He was young—in his first year out of medical school, I think. As he excitedly shared his plans to reinvent himself, I was equally in awe and fascination at my own gifts, and terrified that his influential parents would hunt me down. *Who on Earth is this twenty-something personal trainer who talked our son into throwing away his whole career? She must PAY!* (P.S. They never did this, but that's where my mind went!)

After that, I tried *really* hard to stick to fitness. I blogged about fitness, nutrition, and fat loss. I branded as a "fitness chick." I created a multiple-six-figure business selling fitness online, long before anyone else was doing anything much on the internet, let alone running a business there. I simply followed my desire to share truth with people and combined it with my other desires: to make money, and to create art from life. I cracked the code on an industry (online marketing) that I had no idea *was* an industry at the time—all by being true to the conversation and communication that I knew mattered.

It's funny how our gifts come out sideways, even when we're trying *really hard* to keep them locked away. No matter what I did, that "press play on your life" stuff just kept busting out of me—and massively shifting things for the people around me.

That little girl from the schoolyard—the one who said, *I can help you*—was finally coming out to play, and there wasn't a damn thing I could do to stop her.

YOU'VE ALWAYS BEEN THIS WAY, TOO

Where did it all start for you?

When I was eleven years old, I picked up my first Tony Robbins book.

It was an original copy of *Unleash the Power Within* that I'd grabbed from my father's office shelf. (Oh, that classic beige 1980s cover. And that *hair!*) But more than Tony's wise words and chiseled jaw, I remember the feeling.

It was a remembrance.

A resonance.

A recognition of *my own soul*. And the full-throttle certainty of, "Oh! *That's* what I'm going to do."

It was definite. A fact. One day, I would impact millions with my words, and be a voice of empowerment and inspiration to guide others who were different—like me—to live their lives authentically and purposefully.

It didn't occur to me to wonder *how* this would happen. It wasn't something I announced to my parents as a potential career path. It wasn't a plan, or a goal, or even an idea. It was a *knowing*.

Soon, I was reading Harry Beckwith, Stephen Covey, Brian Tracey, and all of the other "godfathers" of personal development. I knew for sure, at eleven years old, that each of these men was *exactly the same kind of person I was*, and that they had come into my life to remind me of that.

I was born with a soul blueprint for who I am.

So were you.

Maybe you have had similar moments of "knowingness" in your personal backstory. Maybe you are still looking for that remembrance. But on a core level, you already know everything you need to know to rock this life. You already *are* everything you need to be.

Deep down, you agree with this. You know it. It's a fact.

But on the surface, you're still trying to conform.

I hear your fears, your uncertainties, your doubts. I recognize the voice that whispers, "Are you *sure* you're good enough? Do you have a damn clue what's coming for you if you're wrong?"

That voice is *not you.*

That voice is NOT YOU.

It was sent to seduce you away from alignment, from purpose, from soul, from *you.* And if you listen, you will literally create your life from fear.

That thing you're supposed to do, that thing that's of your soul, the thing that will build a movement and attract thousands and make you millions—you already know what it is. You've just gotten really fucking good at ignoring it.

The path of the Rebel Millionaire is about remembrance.

If you pause for long enough to let this sink in, your truth will become obvious. It's so much a part of you, and rooted so deep, that it can't be shaken or swayed or stripped from you. Even if you've spent years being conditioned away from your inner knowing—being told you're too much, inappropriate, delusional, or just plain weird—your truth is still there, waiting for you to live it.

The thing is, we've been schooled to fear, blame, and shame. At every turn, we're told to follow the "right" way—to do things correctly, or else. In this space, our natural and fully expressed selves will never be enough, because it's impossible for something unique to also be "normal." Everything we do or achieve must come at a massive cost of sacrifice, settling, and compromising against our own souls.

Some of the most prominent people in your life fed you this bullshit during your formative years without any of you even knowing what was happening. It happened without you even noticing, let alone questioning. It just sank in.

It's insidious. Treacherous.

Ridiculous.

There's no need to beat yourself up about this, or to be angry or upset at anybody who passed this fear-led messaging on to you. How does that serve you, or anybody else? None of you understood what was happening.

But you understand now—and so you have a choice. You can stay subscribed to the bullshit that keeps you speeding away from your truth, or you can opt out.

Unsubscribe. Delete.

Thank you, goodbye!

And, just like a pesky marketer who keeps popping back up in your inbox even after you've opted out, it will come back. Unsubscribe again. *This shit is not part of you. It's something you choose into—or choose out of.*

I'm not suggesting that you don't have work to do, healing to dive into, and endless layers of new remembrance to, well, remember. The growth only stops when we die, and it won't always be easy. But in the meantime, you don't need to buy into the mindset that you need to be "fixed" before you're allowed to be fully you and live your damn life. Because here is the truth—

Being who you are—who you have always been—is your God-given responsibility. If you don't use the gifts you were given, you will feel like God and life have thrown you aside. Despite all your wins and successes, nothing will fill you up.

Your backstory doesn't have to write your future.

So, the only question left is ...

Are you willing? And will you start now?

Was that a yes?

Fabulous. It's time to unleash the madness.

LET IT BE AWKWARD ...
AND WAIT FOR THE GOLD

For so long, I didn't own my superpower. I dreamed about it, I longed for it—but I felt I just *couldn't* write and speak into the idea of living purposefully. I was a fitness guru. Who the hell would listen to my ideas on life?

But that knowingness, that soul certainty, had sunk its claws into me, and it wouldn't let go.

In 2012, I decided it was time to take the leap. I rebranded under my own name, and decided it was time to be the *real* me. The full-on, unapologetic me who inspired others to live into their truths.

I thought I would create something magnificent.

Instead, I somehow switched from surface-based fitness coaching to surface-based business coaching. How did that happen? Once again, I was teaching nuts and bolts and strategies, with a sprinkle of "be fully you and own it."

I put out offer after offer about living your dream life, being all of who you are, doing the real work ... and they all fell flat. Soon, I was back to being shitty at the world (and myself) for *not listening to or wanting the truth.*

But it wasn't the world.

It was <u>me</u>.

I wasn't owning it. I didn't know how to fully express it. I was back to being that awkward kid on the schoolyard. I wanted to shout from the rooftops, but I was hiding in the bushes again.

What I learned was that the way is only ever revealed through action. You have to commit before the path will appear. You're leaping, stepping, leaning in, trusting, even when you can't see and you don't know.

In the end, you will be who you always were. You can't be anything else—but you *can* choose not to remember. You *can* choose to keep your soul locked up like a prisoner of war. You *can* choose not to become, and not to show up.

And if you wait to be "sure"—if you wait for clarity, or for it to feel easy—you will never begin.

You don't get to mastery, to flow, to owning your "thing," without going through the awkward, the clumsy, the gangly, and the "Oh, my God, I look like an idiot."

You don't get to race up the stairs like a gazelle, barely breathing hard, totally on fire while everyone else stares at you in awe, without first pushing through the pain, the discomfort, and the "get me the fuck out of here."

Just one step, then another. Keep going. Learn. Fall down. Lean into the pain. Feel the fear. Get up and go again. Get stronger. Get faster. And eventually …

Flow like the fucking wind.

Most of the people who knew me as a kid would be shocked at the way I play these days. The way I know my place in the world and *claim* it, publicly. The way I create incredible outcomes at the flick of a switch. The way I make millions just by being me. The 2012 version of me probably would have been shocked, too. I'm so far beyond where she was, and I climbed so many flights of stairs to get here, I can barely touch her anymore.

But still, I am who I always was. This version of me was always here, waiting.

I just stopped apologizing for her.

I stopped shoving her out of sight behind the bushes.

Instead, I said "Fuck, yes!" to everything she was, and everything she stood for, and cranked up the volume.

YOU GOTTA DROP
THE BACKSTORY

If there is a "secret strategy" to claiming your true identity as a Rebel Millionaire, it's this: You have to drop
your backstory. You know, the one you tell yourself
about not knowing who you are and what you really
want—and how your whole life to date has been proof
of this not-knowing.

That story is bullshit.

You've *always* known how to be that fully-expressed
version of you. You know how things work for you—
and how they don't. You know how to take action at the
precise moment it's required.

All those times things didn't work? They were the
times when *you didn't listen.* They were the times when
you chose not to be you because it was easier, or more
acceptable, to go along with the crowd. They were the
times when you filtered, dialled down, adjusted, or simply hid in the bushes.

Think about it.

If you had just been you—all of you, without filters
or apologies—you wouldn't have been pulled this way
and that, or said yes when you should have said no.
You would have *known* what to do and how to stay on

track. In fact, you probably *did* know—but you were so wrapped up in trying to "do it right" that you missed it.

There are no requirements to becoming a Rebel Millionaire except one: you need to do it as your whole self.

Only then will you be able to break away from the continual fear, judgment, and other nonessential bullshit that keeps you thinking the whole world is about to come crashing down on you, or that some made-up deity is going to pop up and say, "Sorry. You're done! We figured out you were just making it up as you go, and you're *out*!"

Only then will you be able to stop the train before it goes off the rails.

Only then will you be able to take action from a place of pure knowing.

Only then will you become a *true* rebel—not someone fighting against the status quo, but someone who has opted out of the whole damn program.

In the end, it really is that simple.

Just. Be. You.

AND NO, YOU DON'T GOTTA HEAL TO STEP UP

There are a whole subset of experts who will tell you that you need to heal something (or, in some cases, everything) before you can reach "success."

They talk about breakthroughs, upleveling, reprogramming, and becoming who we need to be to reach our goals. All of that is fantastic. I'll nod along.

But then, just when things are getting good, they say something like, "You'll *never* get to where you want to go if you don't do [insert modality here]." Usually, this happens right before the sales pitch.

Whenever someone starts talking that way, I lose interest immediately.

Believe me, I know all about healing. I know all about breakthroughs. I love them both. But I don't respond to fear. It's like negotiating with a terrorist—and I'm simply not available for that.

I know that the moment I let that fear in—the moment I say, "I can't have what I want because I'm not there yet"—the game is over.

Everything you need is already inside of you. Do you have some shit to deal with? Sure—we all do. Will you become a new version of you as you fly like a bat out of hell toward the thing you want? Of course. But none of that needs to wait for you to be "healed," or even ready. It all gets to happen *now*, just because you choose it. Whatever you see inside of you is *fully available*, regardless of what you've endured in your life, the trauma you've suffered, or what other people or institutions have done to and around you. The whole "deal and heal" thing can happen simultaneously to your expansion. It's not cause and effect. After all, you're letting life move through you. You're letting *God* move through you—and God already knows what's happening behind the curtain. You don't need to tidy up your internal closet before you earn permission to begin.

The point is, following fear won't get you there.

You don't have to give fear a voice. In fact, if you're serious about creating aligned success in your life, you should have a personal policy of *not* giving it a voice—and that means not letting others, even mentors and gurus, give it a voice either.

Remember: *Nobody* knows better than you what is right for you.

I want you to promise me—and, more importantly, promise yourself—that you will never let anyone convince you that you need something beyond what is already inside you to get what you want.

The only thing you need in order to move forward from here is *your own decision to move forward*. Your decision to show up as your fully-expressed self. Your decision to step into the "baby deer" space and be willing to splat on the floor if that's what it takes to remember who you are and why you're here.

So if, while reading this chapter, you had any thoughts like, "This is all great, Kat, but I still need to heal X in order to *really* stop my train and claim my inner knowing," understand that this is your *chosen* backstory, and it's time to let it go. Part of the "remembering" is understanding that there is not a single person, text, modality, knowledge base, practice, or time frame that you require in order to do this work. That does not mean you can't—or won't—choose those different pathways of growth and exploration, or those ways of doing business, or those ways of life. But they are pathways you *get* to choose. Not "have to" choose.

Nothing outside of you is a gateway to what's inside you. The very idea makes no sense. So ...

There is no magic bullet. There is no missing link. There is only, and has only ever been, you.

You are ready.

And when you truly decide to have what you want, you will *always* get it.

That is not to say you can't ask for help. But learning because you feel *inspired* is different than learning because you feel *deficient*. One comes from soul, the other from fear.

I've met and been guided by some truly amazing and powerful people in my life: mentors, friends, healers, energy workers, and people who have gifts spanning far beyond this physical world. People about whom I can truly say, "This person changed my life."

But not a single part of me believes that, had I not met or said yes to those people, I wouldn't be where I am now. I am where I am, and who I am, *because I chose it.* The people who helped me weren't the reason I succeeded. God put them in my path because I had already made the choice, and their support and guidance matched what was already bubbling up within me.

So don't give fear a ticket to ride your train. Don't give lack, or scarcity, or the crazy idea that you're broken a seat on that motherfucker. Be courageous, and discerning, and above all ...

Follow the "Fuck, yes."

CHAPTER 3

YOU DON'T NEED PERMISSION

B efore I understood that everything I needed was already inside of me, and that I could build a business and make millions of dollars from soul, I did a pretty good job of being half-assed at building a business that made *some* money and helped *some* people.

Maybe that's me being a bit harsh on myself. In fact, it definitely is. But when you have something big inside you, and you don't let it out fully, everything else feels like a shadow version of creating.

Back in those pre-letting-out-all-my-crazy days, I was good—even great—at what I did. I worked my ass off, so clients got results, money was made, and people got paid. ("People" mostly meaning my first few virtual assistants and the various mentors and consultants I hired, because I hadn't yet realized the value of actually paying *me*. The idea of having breathing room, let alone extra cash, seemed outrageous at the time.)

Everything that was "supposed" to happen was happening. Yet, it was clear that I had a firm ceiling in place. Especially after I switched from fitness to business coaching, I felt handcuffed all the time. I kept thinking, "I work so hard. I'm so consistent. Shouldn't something have changed by now?"

So, I knuckled down and worked harder—but it didn't really make a difference. In fact, it seemed like I was slipping right back down the hill I'd spent so long trying to climb.

I felt broken. Tired. Worn down. And so, *so* frustrated, because I knew there was more to me—and to life— than this.

I was also scared. I hadn't yet learned to deny my fear a seat at the table. (Another thing I didn't yet know I was allowed to do!) Money was a constant noose around my neck. My debt was out of control. Most days, I felt like I couldn't breathe.

I did everything I saw others doing to create success. I paid the best business coaches I could find—and since we're talking about the era before online business support was a thing, I had to hunt those badasses down! I bought *all* the programs on success, money, purpose, and business management. I've always been a good student, and creating my business and my dream life wasn't going to be any different. I connected all the dots—and then put a cherry on top, just to be safe.

Honestly, I was exhausted, running scared, and living from my own not-enoughness. But I was willing to keep going. It wasn't like I knew another way to be!

I'm sure it won't come as a surprise when I tell you that, despite following every system avidly, doing precisely what I was told, and giving it my all ...

Nothing changed. I was still slogging up the same hill.

It was torment.

There were times when I was quite literally curled in the foetal position on my floor, sobbing as though the world was ending. Times when I refused to talk about money with my then-husband, Enzo, because the shame I was feeling felt unbearable. Times when I yelled at our then-two-year-old daughter for asking for a treat, because the truth was I didn't have the two dollars to buy it. Times when I met friends at a café and ordered tap water because I couldn't afford a coffee, and I didn't want to assume that they could or should (or would) pay for me. Times (*so* many times!) when I had to put groceries and diapers and gas on my credit cards because otherwise we would go without—and times (too many to bear) when those credit cards would fail at the checkout for those groceries and diapers and gas, because some part of me found it easier to run the gauntlet and hope the card would go through instead of checking the balance beforehand.

But throughout it all, no matter how bad things got— and no matter how close I actually came to moving back in with my parents—the truth was, I still *believed*.

I believed I would break through.

I believed that this wasn't the end of my story.

I had made a choice to walk this path, and I would walk it until my fucking feet bled and I had to crawl on my knees. Because I was born for more.

And then, after months or maybe years of this soul-grinding awfulness ...

I surrendered.

I stopped giving a fuck, because I literally had nothing left.

I let go of all my fear about how others would perceive me. I stopped wondering if my ambitions were warranted, or if they even made sense. I stopped worrying about the money, because there was fuck-all I could do about it anyway.

I let it all go.

And then, I *remembered*.

"HAVE TO" WAS NEVER MEANT TO BE A THING

When I was about twenty-two, my life coach said something to me that was an absolute game-changer—at least, once I finally got my head around it completely, which took about fifteen years.

What I should say is, I "got it" right away, but it took

fifteen years for me to back myself enough to *choose* it.

I saw this life coach every two months or so for a two-hour session. She was a psychologist, best-selling author, and executive life coach, and usually mentored CEOs of major corporations. Her office was a super-stylish two-bedroom apartment with amazing views over downtown Melbourne.

Every time I walked in there, I thought to myself, *This is what I will do one day. I'll sit in my stunning 'office-apartment' with a top-notch coffee machine, surrounded by books I wrote and comfy couches, and I'll just ... help people. And kick their asses. Obviously.*

I still wonder what she thought of me, walking timidly through her door in my personal training uniform and gym-branded fanny pack, and with no real intention or clue why I was there, except that ... I had to be.

I always understood the power of putting myself in a space of upleveling, even when I wasn't quite sure what I was upleveling *into*. To this day, it is one of my favourite truths to come back to, particularly when I feel overwhelmed, stuck, or have no idea how I'm gonna get somewhere.

My coach's hourly rate at the time was $750 for her executive clients, which was absolutely crazy to me at that point in my life. (Bear in mind, this was also over twenty years ago.) She charged me $350 per hour, which was still a stretch for me to pay. I never asked for the discount, or why it felt aligned to her to give it.

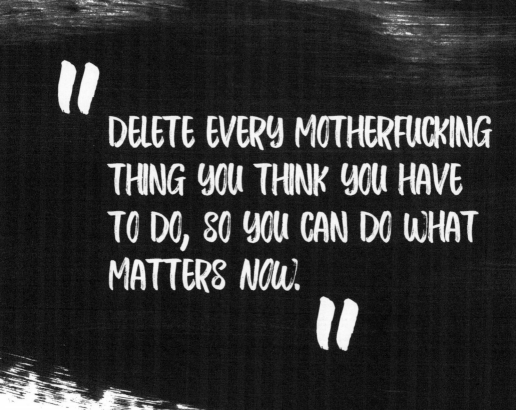

I just said yes, and was grateful. I was absolutely willing to lean into that stretch—and proud of myself, too. I couldn't *not* do it.

My coach and I would sit there and just talk. About my dreams, wishes, and wants. About what was going down in my business at the time. About writing, and speaking, even though I wasn't really doing either of those things at that point.

One day, I broke down and shared how utterly overwhelmed I was feeling around my personal training business. I had nine apprentice trainers working under me, seven of whom were male. They were all incredible trainers and fast learners, each crushing it in their own way. But sometimes, they were also like a bunch of overgrown teenagers (they were actually young adults, but it felt this way!) who would oversleep and then roll in five hours late to work, quite possibly wearing yesterday's stinky clothes.

My role was to support them to build their businesses, and coach them out of their own overwhelm and self-doubt. Some of the boys were particularly ... boyish about it, and I was frustrated. I already had a million things coming at me in my own business, and now I had to manage other people's drama. It was too much!

"I think I need to get more organized," I sighed. "I can't keep up with my to-do list. I feel like I'm drowning."

My coach looked at me, utterly relaxed in her powerful knowing. "Katrina," she said, "What if you just deleted the list?"

I stared at her, speechless.

"What if you simply trusted that, even if you had no list, ever, you would always know what mattered and needed to be done, and that you would be the kind of person to do it?"

I could instantly see what a power move this would be. I could fully see and feel the logic and the freedom of it. And I knew I had that level of faith ... somewhere.

But I didn't follow through. I guess I had more learning to do.

Fast forward about five years. I was at dinner with Charles Poliquin, a world-famous Canadian strength coach (and arguably one of the greatest men of all time in the health and fitness world) who became a long-time mentor and eventually a friend of mine. We were with a group of students who'd taken a class with him that day. As we ate our Thai food, I nervously noticed every move I made, because I was sitting right next to him and was torn between deep admiration and total intimidation.

Charles had only met me that week, but he seemed to see right through me. He said—in the fantastic French-Canadian accent I would come to know and cherish over the years until his passing —"You're the kind of person who needs to live without a list."

I almost choked on my chicken cashew stir-fry.

"You just need to designate Mondays as your 'do everything' day, and spend the rest of the week making it up. This is essential for someone like you to be happy and let your best work flow."

I felt what he was saying in my core. I *knew* it was true. But did I live into it this time?

Nope.

I said I would do it. I agreed that it made sense. But then I did that thing that most people end up doing for their whole damn lives.

I didn't do what I knew I *must*. I didn't choose in faith.

Instead, I stayed in fear.

Maybe I didn't fully understand yet that faith was a choice. That being me was the most viable option.

Fast forward to about 2015. I was totally collapsing, and I felt like I was dragging my husband and daughter down with me. And, at long last, I'd reached that epic tipping point of no longer giving a fuck.

I opened my to-do list—that endless list of things I "needed" to do in order to be the person who could have what I wanted and finally "get there." I opened my email and messaging inboxes. And with my eyes clenched tightly shut, I found the button with my fingertips and—

I deleted the entire fucking thing.

Blank. Slate.

It was scary and exhilarating at the same time. It was free-fall.

It was about bloody time.

I was so sick of being bound to the idea that I always had to be *doing*—that if I didn't follow through on every little thing, it would all come crashing down. I was sick of waiting for the day when I finally did enough that I could get rid of all the "shoulds," and just *be*.

So, let me ask you:

Are all of those routines, rituals, disciplines, and practices that you "need" to do every day (or worse, don't do, and then feel guilty for not doing) actually helping you? Or are you just following the script someone gave you? Are you terrified that if you drop those to-dos that things will fall apart? Or do you feel like being organized gives you more control, even if the endless *doing* stresses you out?

Maybe your to-do list is a good thing for you, even a great thing.

But maybe, just maybe, the real you, the soul you— the "Fuck, yes! and flow" you who is already there and doing the damn thing by being the damn thing—doesn't live like that.

If you were already the person you're working so hard to be—and who you're currently keeping at arm's length—how would you do life?

Me? I'd make every day a blank slate. Every day would be a dance with God and life, which I can't possibly know or anticipate until it unfolds with me inside it. And every night, when I laid my head on the pillow, I would say, "Girl, you did good."

Because here is the truth—

You don't have to earn your life.

You can be trusted to walk it right.

So plant your eyes, heart, and mind where your soul is pointing you—

And delete every motherfucking thing you think you have to do, so you can do what matters *now*.

YOU WERE NOT BORN TO BE SOME BORING AF STEPFORDPRENEUR

If you're like most people, you've spent your whole life being told who you can and cannot be.

If you're an entrepreneur, particularly in the online space, you will also spend most of your business life being told who you can and cannot be, and what you should and should not do if you want to make money, be "on purpose," and change the world.

When I reached that place of energetic rock bottom, I realized that *no part of me* wanted to do business in the way I was being told to do it. Not a single bit of it spoke to me. Nothing in my heart leaped for joy. No cell in my body was expanded. No "Fuck, yes!" moments were experienced, and no angels came down from heaven to sing me on my way.

And yet, I tried to do it anyway.

Because ... because, well ...

Because people I respected said I should.

Because it seemed like something that made logical sense, and I thought it would (or could, or should) unfold into something.

Because everyone else was doing it that way. Some of them were even succeeding.

Because nobody ever told me that I could unapologetically back myself, go all in on being me, delete the to-do list, give the system the middle finger, and do only my soul-driven purpose work in any way I felt like doing it.

No one told me.

And so, I spent years trying to follow the system—to be a good little marketer, a good little online salesperson, a good little straight-A student.

And meanwhile, my soul—and my bank account—started to wither and die.

If you've ever seen the movie *The Stepford Wives*, you'll remember the kooky plot where visionary, passionate humans are turned into obedient, prim, polished cyborgs by a vengeful Glenn Close. It was both totally kitsch and utterly terrifying. I only watched it once, but it's stayed with me ever since.

I feel like everywhere I look I see this movie playing out in real time—and particularly in the entrepreneurial

"WHEN THE SOUL GOES, SO DO THE MONEY FLOWS."

space. Free-thinking creatives are being transformed by relentless marketing and "get rich quick" strategies into soulless Stepfordpreneurs, largely because no one has yet told them *they are allowed to fully back themselves.* By trying to imitate people who have "made it," rather than choosing what actually feels aligned for them, they're buying into the program.

When I was doing things the way "they" told me to do—or, rather, what I let myself believe was required for success—I wasn't attracting my soulmate clients. I wasn't doing the work I was called to do. And I was not letting all of who I was be seen. Really, then, was it any surprise that I wasn't creating the business, the life, or the *me* that I came here for?

Truth? I don't regret a second of it. I learned what I needed to learn—to listen to my inner knowing, stop pretending I wasn't ready, and delete the damn to-do list. This time, the learning stuck, because I had first-hand experience of *exactly* how awful the alternative could be.

This isn't to say that "bro marketing" strategies and by-the-book business structures won't work for you as a Rebel Millionaire. Some will be a perfect match to what your soul wants. These will feel like a "Fuck, yes!" Others will feel like a "maybe." Many will feel like a flat-out "Hell, no!"

Where we go wrong is in thinking that the maybe—or the "Hell, no"—will somehow turn into a "Fuck, yes!" if we follow the program for long enough.

That's where the Stepfordpreneur journey begins. *Just conform and do as you're told. It will all work out. You'll see.*

Delete, delete, delete.

OWN YOUR AWESOME

When you decide to opt out of the Stepford (aka zombie) life, you'll figure out that so much of what once seemed "authentic" is anything but.

The second you start to think about growth strategies, growing your following, getting visible, or any of the things people tell you to do to get your "thing" out there in the world, you make it impossible to reach your goal as the fullest, most authentic version of you.

Yup. Funnels, optimizing, ads, launches, sales pages, emails ... the whole damn thing will literally switch off your ability to receive with ease and effectively create the real work of your soul.

Of course, a lot of people would probably disagree with me on this. Maybe you do, too. Maybe you still think that following the rules is the only way to get it working—and then, maybe, once you are making money and are out of debt and have the cars and the house and the things, you can pull out that passion again.

Not too much, mind. That might stop things working. After all, we need to give the people what they want to buy.

I happen to have an inside view of the world of the Stepfordpreneur and know a lot of people at the top. And I can tell you that, behind the scenes, many people who appear to be killing it with their "freedom-based laptop lifestyles" are miserable as hell. Not all the time. Not in every area of life. But in a general sense. They often ask me, "What's going on? Is this all there is?"

I'll tell you what's going on.

Soul. Fucking. Emptiness.

Okay, okay, maybe it's not *that* dramatic! But actually? Maybe it is. After all, you're either flowing, creating, and monetizing within alignment, or ...

You're not

And if you're not? We're talking a life devoid of deep connection to purpose, self, and little things like that.

No big deal.

So even if conformity worked—which, most of the time, it doesn't—and you actually got away with building that basic-bitch-business-in-a-box, you *still* wouldn't have what you really want.

I've been there. Every single one of my high-end clients has been there. They are artists, messengers, creators, soul-driven leaders ... and they were trying to be Stepfordpreneurs.

What I and my clients experienced every time we forgot this truth was this:

When the soul goes, so do the money flows.

True success—the way you've always known it can be—comes from being you and following your soul. When you do this—for real, not just on Instagram—it's literally impossible not to get results. The other way? Not so much.

You can either believe this, or you can keep looking for the magic stairway to straight-A-student heaven, and climb it until you fall off the side *because it never goes anywhere.*

So please.

Own your awesome.

Be unapologetic about whatever you want to put out there in the world.

Speak from your soul and keep showing up. Be a shining example of full-blown badassery, and let them *feel* you.

KNOW THIS: THERE'S NO COMING BACK

You are worthy.

Your work helps people beyond what they can put into words. When you're in soul alignment, people are shifted just by being in your presence.

You know it. Deep down, you know it.

And yet, part of you is terrified to fully own this huge power, presence, and potential. Why? Because once you make that commitment to own your awesome, there's no coming back from it.

No part of you is actually scared to be you. But if you were to expose your actual soul—not the almost-convincing shadow version you've been waving around like a flag—people would see it. They'd see *all* of you— and once they saw you, they'd never want to see anything less from you.

You couldn't hide in the Stepfordpreneur tactics. You couldn't distract yourself with to-do lists. You'd have to focus all day, every day, on *being you*—all of you. On purpose.

When you claim your soul truth, by default, you refuse to be available for anything *other* than that. You refuse to lie to yourself anymore. You refuse to see yourself as broken, or in need of fixing, or "not there yet." You decide that you will not get out of bed each day until you have dug in and pulled out a raw, bloody chunk of your truth to share with the planet.

You will never again make a choice unless it's a full, "Fuck, yes!" with goosebumps and shivers. Even when you "should." Even when it pisses other people off.

You will never fake it. You will never speak half-truths or polish shiny objects and Instagram photos for mass consumption.

That's what is in store for you when you unleash the real you on the world.

Are you ready?

Because we are tired of waiting.

CHAPTER 4

DESIRE

*Y*ou know what is just next level certified and laminated bullshit? Feeling shame and guilt for spending three bucks on a coffee.

When you're living dollar to dollar (or cent to cent), you kind of get used to never having money. I know I got used to feeling that noose around my neck—and, on a not-so-sidenote, I also got addicted to the adrenalin rush of "will I or won't I survive another day?" But eventually, even for the most die-hard, thrive-on-danger-preneurs, being broke as fuck gets *old*.

I was broke as fuck for what felt like an eternity. Even when my business started making money, I spent it all on business "opportunities" that led me further and further away from where—and who—I wanted to be. I let big things like taxes and student loan debts slide, which only made the problems worse. And, somehow, I had convinced Enzo that our family could live off my business (if, by live, you mean never breathe or relax again), so it was all on me.

On the one hand, I was making multiple five figures a

month—and, at the same time, carrying over a hundred grand in debt. I was literally haemorrhaging money. The only thing that stopped me from giving up and declaring bankruptcy was that I was too proud to let go of my title of "Director" of my company. You can't be a director if you're bankrupt.

The thing was, I *knew* what I wanted. For so long, I'd been talking and dreaming and *knowing* that I would one day live an incredible life. I *knew* I was born for more. I *knew* I was here to make millions, impact millions, unleash my true message on the world, and change lives.

I wanted freedom. I wanted choice. I wanted to speak my truth and share my message with the world without filters or strategies. I wanted to have everything I wanted *my* way—and be fully supported the whole time.

But I was still waiting for someone to give me the formula for being me "out there" in the world.

I did everything my mentors and coaches told me— and all of it took me further away from what I actually wanted. Every dollar I made felt like a struggle—but I'd made the investments, and done the work, so I had to keep going, right?

Well, no—but that's also not the point.

I wasn't still broke because I wasn't "ready" to be rich yet. I wasn't still broke because I had more inner work to do, or because I hadn't joined the right programs with the right people. I wasn't still broke because I didn't have the right high-level offers in place, or because I wasn't coaching with the right people.

I was still broke because I hadn't *decided* to stop being broke. Just because I had a destiny didn't mean it would come to fruition.

One day in January, 2014, I woke up sick of it all.

I was done. Done with my own bullshit. Done with the shame, and the guilt, and the lack of good coffee. Done with not being able to buy and have and do whatever I chose, whenever I chose, without worrying about the price tag.

I was clear about what I wanted. But just because the dream was there, and just because I had faith it was coming to me, didn't mean it would actually happen.

I had to *choose* it first. And I had to mean it. Because if I really decided and believed, I would let go of all the other options—including the option to be (and stay) broke.

That day, I decided to be done with not being rich as fuck. Money rich. Spiritually rich. Energetically and emotionally rich. Time rich.

Of course, what immediately came up was, *Am I really good enough? Have I done enough? Am I worthy? Is it truly my time? Can I be that lucky? Do I still have more to learn?*

ENOUGH!

No more questioning.

No more asking "how" or "when."

No more waiting.

Later that morning, I sat my ass down in a beachside coffee shop (which, coincidentally, is not far from where I'm writing this now), ordered a triple shot long macchiato, took out my journal, and started to write.

Honestly, I'm not sure where the idea came from; I guess soul just led it out of me. Without fully realizing what I was doing, I began to write the story of how I had snapped my so-called "future" into the now and become money-rich overnight.

I wrote as if it was already May of that year, and I was looking back on the previous four months. (Why did I pick four months? Why the fuck did I put on black panties this morning instead of red? I have no idea. Because I did.)

What I wrote was a very clear, very specific tale of how I had gone from being continually broke and in debt, with money slipping through my fingers no matter how much I made, to *all of a sudden* having tens of thousands of dollars show up out of nowhere, like magic. I wrote about how ideas and creativity had flowed forth from me, and how everything had changed on a dime. I wrote about the energy and emotion of this crazy shift, and how grateful and excited I'd been when it all happened.

Most of all, I wrote about how all of this had come about as a result of me *deciding* to get over my broke-ass bullshit and be rich instead.

In the story, I marveled (and asked the reader to

"

IMAGINE IF YOU CHOSE TO
BELIEVE THAT WHATEVER
YOU SEE AND FEEL INSIDE
YOU IS REAL.

"

marvel with me) at just how quickly and effortlessly it had all happened.

It was one of the greatest testimonies I've ever written or read about just how fast things can change when you say yes to soul and start playing life outside the Stepfordpreneur paradigm. When I was done writing, I could barely believe what had poured out of me.

But wait, there's more.

I then *published* said story on Amazon as part of my "Think Like a Rich Chick" series. On the day it came out, I was still skint. Be mad at me if you want. But the fact is, what I was teaching in the story matched up *exactly* with this strategy. It's all about planting yourself in the energy of what you know will happen, and then consciously choosing to live from what is energetically true, regardless of whether it has physically occurred (yet). It's a matter of "pulling out" or "leaning into" existing realities in order to allow them to transpire.

After I pressed "publish" on that story, I honestly forgot about it. I was already on to the next thing.

Then, I decided that Enzo, my kids, and I were going to press play on an adventure that was long past due. We would be officially location-free for the next two years—the exact thing I'd planted in my mind as a possibility way back when I started blogging! In April, we did it. I booked the tickets for a journey I had no idea how to afford beyond the first weeks. I spent my last saved dollars (literally) on our one-way flights to

Munich, where we'd be starting our travels, two babies underfoot.

To me, this choice to go to Europe with no extra money, no real plan, and two toddlers to care for wasn't crazy. It was a matter of following my soul, and it had been bubbling up from within me for years at that point. I knew we were meant to go. I was unavailable to *not* go, whether or not I had money to live on. I could just as easily be perpetually head-barely-above-water in Europe as at home—so why not lay myself on the line for what I was guided to do? I had decided to be done with where I was; it was time to relentlessly move forward as though I actually *believed* I would get where I said I was going.

Fast forward one month.

Almost as soon as we'd landed in Germany, shit just *blew up*. Money came in out of nowhere, as if by magic—to the tune of me receiving over $50,000 in cash in four weeks.

The month after that, I made $70,000. The month after that, $80,000. And by December of that year, I had my first $100,000 month. Since then, my income has only ever dipped below six figures per month one or two times.

I don't know exactly when I remembered the story I had written—but when I did, it blew my mind. I had written very specifically about how money would come in, and I'd even given a timeline—within four months of my decision to be done with being broke. Back in January, I had written the exact story of how things went down that summer, as though it had already happened. When I re-read what I had written, it was exactly—and I mean *exactly*, right down to the last little chill-inducing bit of it—what had happened in real life.

I had written about what I longed for—what I was being shown was available. What I had *decided*, on that January day, to have.

And then, once I followed through on the (often terrifying) actions I was guided to take, it all came true. Obviously.

Your soul really does know the way.

IT'S TIME TO CHOOSE

Since that day in the coffee shop, when I wrote my vision of wealth while sipping a latte I technically couldn't afford, I have understood the incredible power of our words.

So many things I have written since that day, small or big, have come to life. I write the things I desire, and what I am shown from God and soul, and then ... they show up. This act of writing what's inside you into reality is one of my favourite things to teach on and share.

But whether or not you're consciously doing this practice (or a similar one) right now, know this:

You *are* writing a story right now that will come to life.

You're writing it with your thoughts. Your beliefs. Your actions. Your words. Those wishes and wants you scribble in your journal every day.

Even if you don't realize it, you are telling a story about what you've *decided* to have, and what you've decided is still out of reach.

Imagine what could happen if you just *wrote the damn story you want to create*, instead of the one everyone tells you is happening.

Imagine if you chose to believe that whatever you see and feel inside you is real.

Imagine if you then followed whatever actions you were guided to take, because you knew the story you were telling would come true—that it had no choice but to come true.

What would happen then?

Unless you've been living under a rock, you've probably done (or at least heard about) "creating a vision." Seeing the big picture. Imagining what you want. Picking a direction. Honestly, I'd be shocked if, by this point, you haven't at least contemplated what your "vision" is.

Let me be clear: vision is not building the brand, selling the product, providing the service, buying the car, or having the cash. Those are *goals*. Goals are great— but if you think that's all there is for you to desire, you have seriously forgotten who you are and what this was always meant to be about.

Your vision is the big picture of *who you came here to be.* That thing that's been calling you from the beginning. The freedom. The joy. The flow. The feeling of doing exactly what you're meant to be doing, every single day—because your soul desires it, or just because you damn well feel like it.

If you really do want the cookie-cutter "vision" of the methodical business, the programmed pathways, and the boring-but-maybe-still-sort-of-effective strategies put out there by boring-but-maybe-still-sort-of-effective people, by all means, keep doing what you're doing.

But if you want to achieve that feeling of being truly *alive*—of living from soul and doing all the stuff you can't and won't shut up about—you're going to have to get off your ass and choose it.

You might think you're already choosing it because you're busy. You get shit done. But, as we've talked about, running toward your dream isn't about being busy. It isn't about checking off the damn to-do list. I mean, good for you that you can tick all those boxes, when some people never get off the couch—but that's not vision. That's not choosing from soul. If your only claim to fame is that you "get shit done," you're falling right into the Stepfordpreneur trap.

If you came here to build a life, to live your soul's calling—and yes, to be rich as fuck—it's time to stop excusing your own bullshit with the "I'm too busy" argument. So what if you're getting shit done? So what if you're marginally more successful than people around you?

So.

Fucking.

What.

You're either chasing the true vision and the dream you came here to fulfill, or you're just really good at filling up your time.

There is no in-between.

ALL YOU NEED IS THE VISION

Of course, things aren't always as simple as saying yes and then forging merrily ahead. Sometimes clarity is *nowhere* to be found—and certainty? Not your friend.

I remember a time—some years down the track from that period of travelling location free—where I felt *all* of the above and was filled with inner turmoil. I decided out of nowhere that it was time to buy a home on the Gold Coast. A house. And, of course, I wanted

" YOUR VISION IS THE BIG
PICTURE OF WHO YOU CAME
HERE TO BE.
"

one in "Millionaires Row," and with some key specifics which were just ... well, not readily available for love or money.

I knew that when I decided what I wanted, it was done. I would get it, and then some. But at the time, I had no idea how that could possibly happen.

I felt like I was trying to make all the pieces of my vague, nonspecific dreams fit together in a way that made sense, like putting together a jigsaw puzzle with a blindfold on. My mind kept shrieking, "What if I fail? What if I just can't pull it off?!"

And then I realised—

It didn't matter *how* I would receive my home. The "how" wasn't important. All that mattered was that I could hold the vision.

I have no idea how I momentarily forgot this, since even back then I was teaching it all the time in business. But sometimes, we *do* forget. We get caught up in the doing, the how, the figuring out of it all—and we stop ourselves in our tracks.

But now, I was clear. I knew what I wanted, and that it was time to choose it. I knew it would come to me.

And come to me it did.

I started looking at beachfront properties with the specific attributes that would make it the perfect home for me and my family. When I found my home (because even before I bought it, it was *my* home), I knew right away that it was meant to be.

Only, the bank didn't agree.

You see, I'd bought an investment property in my home state for just under $1,000,000 just a few months before and had cleaned out all my cash and savings. As a result, the bank—with whom I'd had a strong relationship for years, and who had literally hundreds of months of my business income on record—decided that the standard deposit amount of twenty percent simply wasn't going to cut it.

Suddenly, instead of looking at a deposit of $390,000, I was being asked to come up with a deposit of $880,000. In *three months*. Even though my business makes amazing money, that's a fuckload of cash to come up with in ninety days. And that was *extra* money. I still needed to meet all my usual payments, payroll, other business expenses, and existing investments. I also refused to compromise on my lifestyle or "cut back" in order to have more. That's simply not how I operate. In fact, I chose long ago to NEVER operate that way.

So, $880,000 in *extra* money it was!

I'd never created anything at that scale before. It was quite terrifying, to be honest.

And yet, *this was my house*—the house I was meant to buy for myself and my babies.

I didn't ask, "Do I dare?" Instead, I asked, "How could I *not* dare, when I'm being clearly shown that this is for me—and when I choose to live by these beliefs and underlying principles?

Did I actually *believe* at the time that I could come up with $880,000 in three months? That was a huge faith leap, even for me. But when I put aside the "Can I ...?" and the "How will I ...?" and the "Oh, my God, is that really possible?"

All I needed to ask was, "Is this aligned for me? Yes or no?"

Clearly, the answer was yes.

That's how you receive from what is already energetically "done." You decide, and God provides. The way is shown—and you, of course, follow it. You do whatever work is required, while also realizing that the *true* work is the inner stuff. The mindset stuff. The faith stuff.

For this to work, you've got to *choose* to have that level of faith. You've got to realize that it *is* a choice, not a feeling. And then, of course, you've got to take aligned action. But if you know your job is to say "Fuck, yes!" to soul, you can *never* not dare.

Once I made the decision, I handed it over.

Letting go of the "how" is central to what I teach, and it's *exactly* and the *only* way I have been able to get here. It started that day in January, 2014 when I decided I was done being broke and wrote the story I published in that early book. I had a clear vision of what would come— but if I had sat down and tried to paint the picture of the business I have now, telling myself I couldn't create or receive or take action without knowing exactly where

I was headed and how it would look ... well, I would never have started.

I broke through because I had a vision and intention for impact, for speaking my truth, for being heard and seen—and, yes, for making millions while living a life of freedom and choice. That was what I knew. And, even when I forgot about the crazy-detailed story I wrote in the coffee shop, I focused on and chose that vision every day.

I held the vision when I had *no fucking idea* what the hell I should be doing, how the money would come, or what would work—which, really, was most of the time.

I held the vision when the things I did that day, that week, or that month didn't work.

I held the vision through all the times I felt like I was *way* off track and needed to start fresh.

The details and the day-to-day focus changed continually, but the vision never left me. So, when you look at what I've created, it's hardly a surprise, is it? I wanted freedom, choice, and the ability to make millions and impact millions—and so, that's what I have. The reality followed the vision as sure as day follows night.

I never said my millions needed to come to me through my online coaching company. I never imagined that I'd attract my dream life by working with a certain number or type of clients. I never imagined that I'd need to hire X person to do X thing, or that I'd need to post exactly this many times on social media before it all "stuck." The details were revealed along the way—and they changed. Sometimes daily.

The details are never part of my vision, because none of the doing is part of my vision. What matters, and has always mattered, is speaking my truth, being heard and seen, and making and impacting millions. There are many ways I could live that. And the way I live and do business will shift and evolve as I continue to live into the vision.

So, when it came to my dream home, as crazy as it seemed, I knew I needed to let go of the "how." Not once did I *try* to come up with the money, sell extra stuff, or engineer a plan around how to make the finances work. That would have been me trying to do God's job. I just trusted that life would step up for me because I was stepping up.

Long story short, the money appeared. I got the house. I moved in—and then claimed and called the fuck in an *additional* $100,000 for the initial luxury furnishings I wanted.

My family and I are beyond happy here. My soul feels alive here. This home is, without a doubt, for me—for us—and it always was. I said yes with *no idea* how I'd make it happen, and all because I understood that it was never about *me* "making shit happen."

See how this works?

You don't need to ask "how."

You don't need to jigsaw your life.

You don't need to worry about what (or who) fits where.

You just need to know what you want and decide to have it.

Then run like the wind to be the person who backs herself that boldly.

THE UTTER CRAZINESS OF IT ALL

Maybe you're thinking, "This is the breakthrough I've been waiting for!"

Or, maybe, you're thinking, "I'm just so glad this stuff works for *you*, Kat, but my life doesn't operate that way." (Cue the list of excuses you've been hanging onto for years to justify why you haven't actually decided to have what you want.)

Here's a little secret for you: You *always* get exactly what you focus on and decide to have. Always, always, always!

What might trip you up is that you haven't stopped deciding (and focusing on) what you *don't* want.

You might be saying, "I don't want to be broke any-

"THAT'S HOW YOU RECEIVE FROM WHAT IS ALREADY ENERGETICALLY "DONE." YOU DECIDE, AND GOD PROVIDES. THE WAY IS SHOWN."

more." Okay, good for you. But have you *decided* to be rich?

You might be saying, "I don't want to be single anymore." But have you *decided* what you want in a relationship?

You might be saying, "I don't want to be a robotic Stepfordpreneur!" But have you *decided* to create a business from soul?

Until you decide to have what you want, you will get what you focus on—which is usually what you *don't* want.

Ditto if you're talking to yourself about what you "should" want, like: "I don't want to be broke, but I *should* be happy with what I have. I'm comfortable. I'm getting by." Or, "I don't want to be single anymore, but I *should* stay single because if I partner up I'll never see my single friends anymore." Or, "I want to build a business from my soul, but I *should* follow this program/coach/formula because other people have made money with it."

Can you see how that won't work, can't work, and is obviously *not working*?

Be still for a moment, right now.

Stop thinking for a moment, right now.

Put your hand on your heart for a moment, right now, and ask ...

"What do I *actually want*?"

Not, "What do I think I *should* want?" Not, "What is

appropriate for me to want?" Not, "What am I allowed to want at this stage of the game." Not, "What do I need to do to get what I want and make it work?" No stories, no attachments. No excuses.

What the fuck do you *actually want?*

If you ask that question sincerely, and give yourself a moment of stillness to get beyond the bullshit, your soul might answer something like this.

I want freedom. I want choice. I want to speak my truth. I want to create my art. I want to change people's lives. I want piles of money. I want loads of free time.

And so on and so forth.

You will always get what you fully choose and focus on. Period. The end.

But even if you don't choose, you're still choosing.

You're choosing "should." You're choosing default. You're choosing the windowless room, the protected bubble, the comfort zone. Nothing you want is there, and you know it.

So stop waiting for clarity to press play on your life. The only moment we can live in is *now.* So why would we try to figure out the future?

Your only job, if you want to live your biggest vision, is simple:

Decide your vision.

Decide that it's done.

And then, take a breath, and take a step in this moment from faith, based on what feels right to you, right now. Not based on outcome. Not based on logic, or some program you've invested in. Just based on the fact that you decided, and now it's done.

That's the craziness of living from soul.

WHEN THINGS WORK, THEY WORK

In November of 2014, I was sitting on top of a washing machine in an RV park near Lake Tahoe. It was 11:00 p.m. and I was freezing my ass off. Every few minutes, I had to get up off the washer and walk around the tiny laundromat because the lights were on a timer and would shut off if I didn't move enough.

As part of our two-years-abroad plan (or non-plan, rather), we were enjoying a month-long RV trip from Pasadena to New York City. Our kids were loving it. And after my crazy month-long expansion that spring, I was living the location-free laptop-lifestyle dream.

Okay, there were a few cracks in the dream. Relationship ones, mostly. There's nothing like living out of a suitcase for months at a time with a couple of kids underfoot to bring relationship stuff to the surface. But although it wasn't perfect, we had done the damn thing. *I* had done the damn thing, and created a business that allowed us to travel the world and be fully supported while we did it.

The idea for this RV adventure had crept up on us gradually. We'd thought, "What a great adventure!" The original plan had been to rent the RV, then pull into a nice hotel every four or five days to fancy it up a little and make the rest of the trip feel less claustrophobic. We had no idea it would be so much fun—although, in hindsight, it probably wasn't the smartest decision to travel across the States in the middle of winter.

As a result of the cold, our RV toilet had to be voluntarily taken out of action. The shower, too. So, it wasn't always the cleanest or nicest-smelling trip, but it was still amazing. I also lost a front tooth (snapped it off on a giant homemade peanut butter cup I'd purchased in Park City, Utah, and which was frozen due to the icy temperatures in our RV) and ended up looking like a total hillbilly for about ten days until I found a dentist. I had also gained some pounds, and ended up dressing almost entirely in sweats from WalMart. Plus, my blond grew out—so, roots for days. (My internet community may or may not have enjoyed some jokes at my expense about how I fit right in with the general vibe of some of the states we were travelling through.)

Overall, it wasn't glamorous, but you know what? It was one of the best times of my life.

So why the heck was I camped out on the laundromat washing machine?

"EVERYTHING INSIDE ME IS REAL. EVERYTHING INSIDE YOU IS REAL, TOO."

I was running a training, of course.

It was Week 3 of my now-signature six-week course, "It's Only Money, Honey: The Business and Money Breakthrough Program for Women Who Want It All, Now, And KNOW They're Gonna Get It." It was a huge deal for me to create this course, and teach from soul about the energy of abundance, receiving, and cold hard cash—not just because it's a hot topic, but because it was a "coming out" for me around my past money struggles. I had finally figured some shit out, and now I was embodying it. More, it was coming through me, and my soul told me it was time.

In under a year, I'd gone from living in constant fear—scared to look at my bank accounts, constantly ashamed because I still didn't have my shit together, constantly worried about being "found out" (for what, I'm not sure. Not being a proper adult?)—to knowing that I could afford whatever I wanted, whenever I *chose.*

I could choose to spend a month in an RV with no working toilet, and spend a frozen night snowed in outside of Tahoe.

I could choose to stay at five-star hotels anywhere in the world.

I could buy the fanciest coffee in town and not bat an eyelash. (Honestly, out of all of it, the coffee felt like the biggest luxury. It *meant* something, you know? It was a statement about who I chose to be.)

And I'd finally dragged my finances out of that head-in-the-sand place and into the woman-who-backed-her-self-and-*expected*-to-be-wealthy space I'd been chasing for years.

I knew I never needed to feel that despair and powerlessness around money again. I had cracked the code. I had chosen to be rich, and my vision had come true in ways I never could have imagined. I was literally a world away from that Melbourne coffee shop now, and things just kept getting better. Now, I had trust that even if I fell down in a big way, I could hold the vision powerfully enough to choose my way out of the hole.

I came home from that trip with the business that would evolve into The Katrina Ruth Show. I had certainty about who I was, as well as who I would be and what I would create. It was done.

I had chosen what I wanted. I had chosen how I wanted it. Then, I'd said "Fuck it" to the rest, because I finally knew the truth:

Everything inside me is real.

Everything inside *you* is real, too.

That's the key to it all. The magic bullet. The thing that makes all your badassery and mind-blowing goals possible—whether those goals involve dominating your industry as a multiple-seven-figure mogul or sitting naked by your pool in Bali and gesticulating wildly at the sky while you get downloads from soul. It's knowing—and believing, with your whole body, mind, and soul—that if you *choose* it, it will come to life.

From here on out, this is your daily commitment: to say yes to soul, to be fully you, and to choose what you want without any excuses, reasons, or exceptions. From today forward, you are *no longer available* for anything less than your biggest vision.

Are you ready to do that?

Are you willing?

Good. It's about damn time.

Success follows certainty. And certainty can only come from your unshakable decision to have what you want. The world will never give you certainty. You have to create it for yourself. Just like Henry Ford famously said in one of my all-time favourite quotes: "Whether you think you can, or whether you think you can't, you're right."

You have a destiny. A purpose. A reason for being here on this planet. In the next chapter, I'll show you how to connect with it and weave it into your daily actions—but you have to *decide* first. So stop trying to magnetize certainty from outside of yourself, and find it within. Fully own that everything—every fear, doubt, excuse, reason, situation, and challenge—can be over-ridden if you just *decide* to be certain.

So, today, lean in and journal on the following statements:

- I trust in my own delusion.

- I trust in the way I am led by soul.

- Whatever I decide is enough, is enough.

- Whatever I decide is done, is done.

- I *always* get what I decide to have.

- I can't get it wrong.

Delusional? Fantastical? Some would say so. They'd shake their heads in woe at these feel-good statements that are supposed to override your "reality."

But that's the whole motherfucking point, isn't it? Since when did *they* do a killer job of creating your dream life, or living the energy and inner "Yes!" of your purpose?

That's right. *They haven't.*

And those grand statements aren't really about the words. It's the charge. The energy that resonates on a soul level. The switch that flips for you when you say them, that shoves you firmly back to where you're meant to be: in the damn driver's seat, making the decisions about how to live *your* life, *for you*, by being all of you.

So the question really becomes ...

- Do you trust your delusions?

- Do you trust your process?

- Do you trust your vision?

- Do you trust yourself to *decide*?

YOUR "HAVE IT ALL" STORY

And so, here we are, at the reality and knowingness that your "have it all" story is simply this:

Decide what you want.

Decide how you want it.

Fuck the rest.

The truth is, deep down, you have a clear vision. You *know* what you want to create. But for some reason, you're making your bullshit story bigger and more compelling than your "I have it all" story.

The truth is, the "have it all" story is always and only ever written by *you.*

Not by the ones who tell you what you "must" do.

Not by the gurus and strategists and celebrity Stepfordpreneurs.

Not by the voices in your head.

You.

So, if you want the million-dollar beach lifestyle, the hot body, the hot car, and the hot business? You can have it—*if you decide.*

If you want the magazine-gorgeous tiny house, the

rich nomad lifestyle, and the passive income empire, you can have it—*if you decide.*

If you want to dominate your industry, show up every day in custom-tailored power suits, and bounce around the world on your private jet, you can have it—*if you decide.*

So, right now, I want you to get your journal and a pen, and ask yourself these powerful questions:

- "What does 'having it all' mean to me?"

- "What emotional states, energies, or vibes of 'me being me' correspond to my version of 'having it all'?"

- "What do I require on a daily basis to live in those emotional states?"

- "What would I be doing right now if I were completely being 'that person'?

- "What things am I giving my time and energy to that don't meet that standard? Of those, which do I need to reframe, reinvent, or just let go?"

- "If I do *only* the things that align with having it all, what results would I have in my life in six months? A year? Five years?"

As you write, focus on your vision, not your agenda. The what, not the how. *Expect* to have what you desire.

Let that commitment pour out of you.

Most of all, be brave enough to look your vision in the eye, and say, "You're *mine.*"

Inhale.

Exhale.

Yes.

I choose this.

This is mine.

Thank you, God.

Amen.

CHAPTER 5

WHAT DO YOU CARE ABOUT?

It seemed like such a great idea at the time.

A few years ago, I was in a rut. I couldn't seem to motivate myself to make the sales calls I needed to be making to hit my targets. No matter how much I promised myself I'd follow up on those warm leads (never mind the cold ones!), I just couldn't seem to do it.

I felt like the least motivated person ever. Day after day, I'd swear, "This is it! I'm going all in!" I knew more sales was the path to more money—and that sales calls were the path to sales. It's all a numbers game, right? My mentors were the best in the world at online sales, and their systems were undeniably effective.

Get leads. Book 'em in. Get on the sales call. Overcome the objections. Follow up. Hit your numbers. Repeat until goals are met.

And, under the surface ...

Push yourself to do the crap you hate. Play cool sales songs as loudly as possible to try to drown out your soul screaming. Tell yourself the end is worth the means.

The thing was, it worked—*if* you worked the numbers.

But, for the most part, I sucked at that. When I actually got on the phone, I was pretty damn good at selling my $8k offer—but mostly I was hyperventilating and flushing bright red over the idea of *having to spend my entire life selling on the phone.*

So, I decided to put myself in a situation where I had no choice but to do the thing I hated. I flew myself, my husband, our children, and my one sales person, Amanda, from our then-hometown of Melbourne up to the Gold Coast for a week of Sales Hustle Extravagance. My logic was that, if we locked ourselves up in a fancy hotel in a beautiful coastal location, we would be inspired and motivated to close a $100,000 sales week.

On the plane, I got all of us jazzed as fuck about this huge week we were going to have. I even wrote down rewards for hitting different levels. I was so sure that if I just created the right environment and made the time and space to sell, I could kick my resistance to the curb and get some serious momentum going.

Well, that first day we all sat down and charted out our leads on a spreadsheet, going through every person we could possibly re-dial. I could already feel my heart starting to sink a little as I looked at the names of people I really didn't want to call again, let alone deal with as clients. *Amanda can do those,* I thought. All this money and fanfare to get us here—I couldn't start already! I felt it, you know? Possibility.

"
I SELL MY SOUL PURPOSE.
I SELL MY ENERGY AND
PASSION. I SELL MYSELF.
"

But underneath that, the truth was the whole thing just felt ... yuck.

I said to Amanda, "Maybe we just need a great play-list to get us going." We spent an hour (okay, two) on that. It was totally next level. But even after we got that sorted, I didn't feel ready to pick up the phone.

"I'm going to walk down to the shops and get us some coffee," I volunteered. "I'll do a Facebook ad and get us some new leads while I'm there. When I get back, we are *so* going all in on this."

Well ... I never came back.

I mean, I did *physically* come back to hang with my family and sleep. Eventually.

But the me who'd been deluding herself and pretending that she was suddenly going to be all gung-ho about traditional sales methods? That gal left the coast permanently. I haven't seen her since.

After I walked out that door on the pretence I would be back soon, I found a popular, trendy café, ordered some fancy single-origin slow-pour kind of thing (the kind I've since come to despise—old school gritty coffee gal all the way here!), and proceeded to do the same damn thing I always did when I knew something wasn't right.

I pulled out my journal. And a few select orange flavoured chocolate balls I'd stashed in my purse for a needed moment like this. (Darrell Lea, if my Aussie peeps are wondering.) I assigned myself five orange balls, which I placed on the coffee saucer. By the time I'd consciously consumed these delicacies, I decided, I'd be clear.

Ever since I wrote my success into creation and sent our family off on a crazy world tour, my journal had been my go-to for creating soul connection. So now, full of frustration and fuming mad at myself for letting it get this far, I let myself get carried away.

All I want to do is write and speak and educate and motivate and empower people to live the life of their dreams, I wrote. It was the same sentence I'd written a hundred—no, a thousand—times before, and have written just as many times since. It's all I've ever wanted to do.

I'd shared this with mentors a few times, even expanded on it, but they typically responded with a gentle (or not-so-gentle) reminder that my goal wasn't tangible, and that "what worked" was getting new leads and following up and making those awful damn sales calls.

I sat, and I wrote, and I raged.

I DON'T WANT TO MAKE FUCKING SALES CALLS! And I don't believe I have to! I just want to write and do what I feel like doing each day—and so THAT IS WHAT I AM GOING TO DO!

When I finally came back upstairs to the hotel room, Amanda had made a few calls and gotten underway with the plan—while I, very clearly, didn't give a fuck.

117

"You don't want to be here, do you?" she asked. "You don't really want to do this."

I guess it was clear to everyone. I was a terrible, lazy entrepreneur who didn't even want to sell her own products. What the fuck was wrong with me? Why couldn't I just get it together and do the damn thing?

I *should!*

I *must!*

I *had to!*

If I didn't figure this out, I'd be broke again, back to living day-to-day and coffee-to-coffee. And yet, I just *couldn't do it.*

My higher self has always been an obstinate bitch. She just flat-out refuses to do shit she doesn't want to do, no matter what carrot is dangled or how much money is promised.

I don't even recall what we all did for the rest of that week. I know I did a lot of escaping—to the pool, to the café, any place I could be by myself to read and write and journal. Amanda might have made a few more calls, but they didn't amount to much. I don't think I wanted them to. I'd energetically checked out for both of us—and really, for my entire business.

I knew I had to start choosing to do things my own way.

Wanna know something I think is really cool? I have not made a *single sales call* since that week—including for my highest-level soul mentoring program, which is priced at multiple five figures a month. No one on my team has made a single sales call either. And yet, I sell all the time.

I sell my soul purpose.

I sell my energy and passion.

I sell *myself.*

(Well, the "what's coming through me" bit.)

And I continue to escape with my most powerful tool for allowing what's in me out: my journal.

Now, years later, I'm living in my dream home on the Gold Coast. The other day, I drove by the hotel where we stayed during that week of failed hustle— or, rather, that week of true dream life activation! It's practically opposite one of my kids' schools—and yet, I never noticed it until recently. I remembered how uncomfortable I was then—how I wanted to run out the door and never come back. I wondered how I ever thought I "had to" do a single thing in my business or my life that didn't feel like a giant "Fuck, yes!" I wondered how I ever thought I was going to do my purpose work, make millions, be happy, and change the world while acting like a soulless Stepfordpreneur and doing things I hated.

No playlist is good enough to gloss over that level of bullshit.

THAT "WANTING" THING

It's time to admit it.

You don't give a fuck—not one, tiny, single little fuck—about making money, getting followers, and proving that you've "made it."

Oh, you *want* all of that. You wouldn't be reading this book if you didn't *want* it. But you don't really *care* about it on a fundamental level. You also don't *need* it.

And here's another thing: The wanting—and the waiting for the wanting to be fulfilled—is deflecting your focus from what you *actually* care about.

Don't believe me? Let's do an experiment.

Say the following aloud, or write it out in your journal:

I make millions and millions of dollars each year. I am building a multi-hundred-million-dollar empire! Millions of people follow me on social media. I am famous. Known. Influential. Yay!

There's nothing wrong with any of that. In fact, maybe it feels good to say it out loud. Maybe it even feels like destiny to you, like it does for me—like it's part of a future that is *abso-fucking-lutely* going to happen.

And yet, isn't there something kind of empty about it? Like, this is all shit you *want*—but it isn't really the end goal.

Making millions is awesome. (No complaints here!) But is that all it means to be a Rebel Millionaire?

When I write about my goals (which, you'll remember from the last chapter, are different from your "have it all" vision), I definitely bring in the money. I'm constantly calling in my next level of income, followers, and fame. But while I'm doing it, something inside of me always reminds me, "Kat, that's not it. You don't *actually care about that.*"

Immediately, I have a powerful recognition of the truth.

There's nothing wrong with wanting all the trappings of success. But the only way to get to that success is to go all in with the *actual* shit I care about, which is helping people be all of who they came here to be, and to not die with their dreams still locked inside them.

The money and power, it represents something. Maybe it's safety. Security. Freedom. Some measurement of self-worth. But for sure, whatever you *actually* want from that money and power is something that money and power can't give you.

I love money. It's awesome to have a lot of it. It's cool to wake up and know that I can do whatever I want, whenever I want, and that my red-bottomed shoe wardrobe is representing with the best of them.

But fulfillment? Freedom? Peace? Happiness?

"THE WANTING—AND THE WAITING FOR THE WANTING TO BE FULFILLED—IS DEFLECTING YOUR FOCUS FROM WHAT YOU ACTUALLY CARE ABOUT."

Those are my values. And I can give them to myself right here, in this moment, even if all the other stuff goes away.

The other morning, I found myself writing, "What do I actually care about?"

The answers?

- *I want to feel lit up from within.*

- *I want to feel charged with super-flow.*

- *I want to feel excited—bubbling over with joy and energy.*

- *I want to feel proud of myself.*

- *I want to feel connected to God, soul, and self.*

- *I want to feel connected to my body, the planet, and the people I love.*

- *I want to know that I'm getting my true work out into the world, letting my message and art be the driving force.*

- *I want to know that I'm getting the fuck out of my own way and showing up for what is coming through me from God and my soul.*

- *I want to know, when my head hits the pillow each night, that I did what I came here to do, and that I let ALL of it out.*

I want to inspire and empower others to press play on their lives and live their dreams while impacting millions.

When I remember what it's really all about for me, I get excited. Lit up. Charged with confidence, creative power, and energy—all the qualities I need in order to then go out there and do the things that my soul is asking of me.

It's a matter of putting first things first.

When I connect to my soul and what it longs for— aka, my values—it becomes obvious what I should be doing every day: writing, speaking, preaching, performing, showing up for my art, and following flow and soul guidance.

Funnily enough—or not—these are also the *exact* things which have allowed me to build the empire I currently have, and which I know will allow me to continue to grow to the next level.

Remember: Vision, not agenda.

It's so easy to get distracted. When you start asking, "How can I get the money? How can I have the fame?" you'll get sidetracked from purpose. You'll fall into Stepfordpreneur territory. You'll replace following your soul's calling with worry about how many fucking likes you got.

It's dangerous to do that.

When you're focused on money and fame, you're not focused on purpose, soul, and truth. And, honestly, you're being inefficient, since the *real* money only ever follows purpose.

If you can be disciplined enough to tune in every day to what actually matters to you, and choose how you flow into each moment, you'll realize that there is never anything you need to do, fix, or change in order to do your work in the world—yet, at the same time, there is always action to take.

BADASS CORE VALUES

We've established by now that being a Rebel Millionaire means saying yes to soul and being all of who you came here to be. But it *also* means knowing and prioritizing your core values—the things that matter more to you than anything else.

When you live in alignment with your values, it's much harder for other people to faze you. You'll care less about what they think you should be doing, or what their ideas of right and wrong look like. You'll break out of that windowless room and start walking your own path according to your own internal guidance system—and that will become your measure of worthiness and success.

Sometimes, you have to sift through the layers of rubbish that fill up your mind to break through to where the beauty lies. Here's a simple journaling exercise to help you find what makes you say, "Fuck, yeah!" Write until you run out of answers—or until you have at least five items for each of the questions below.

1. Answer as many times as you can: "It is important to me to be _____"

For example, you might write:

- It is important to me to be honest.

- It is important to me to be healthy.

- It is important to me to be energised from within.

- It is important to me to be loving.

And so on.

2. Answer as many times as you can: "It is important to me to be known for _____"

For example:

- It is important to me to be known for helping others live their best lives.

- It is important to me to be known for my generosity.

● It is important to me to be known for my positive attitude.

And so on.

3. Answer as many times as you can: "It is important to me to _____."
For example:

● It is important to me to share my beliefs about living your best life.

● It is important to me to spend time with my children each day.

● It is important to me to exercise daily.

● It is important to me to write daily.

And so on.

4. Answer as many times as you can: "_____ is important to me." This is where you just go nuts! Don't think in terms of what you want to "be" or "do", just think about what is important to you. Answer *at least* ten times.
For example:

● Financial freedom is important to me.

● Working from a place of focus and flow is important to me.

- Being true to myself in my business is important to me.

- Tithing is important to me.

- Freedom is important to me.

- Spontaneity is important to me.

- Choice is important to me.

And so on.

And, just like that, you have your summary list of values. In fact, if you do the exercise above to the fullest, you should have at least twenty to thirty clear values to work with!

The next and final part of this activity is to prioritise the values you uncovered. So, let's put your values in order, from most to least important, until you have a list of fifteen core values to live by. (Why fifteen? Because more than fifteen values is likely to feel like way too much to juggle, and when you live by your *highest* values each day, the rest will naturally fall into alignment.)

Here's how to find your most important value.

Take a look at all the values you identified in the previous exercise. Compare the first one and the one below it. Gut feel: Which one matters most?

Then, compare the winner with the third on the list.

Gut feel: Which do you care about more? Continue comparing all the way through your list. Whichever value wins is your number one core value.

Write that value down at the top of a new list and start the process again for your number two value. If at any time you're struggling to choose, ask yourself: if I knew I could never have one of these values, which would I let go?

When you're done, you should have a clear list of values in order of priority.

Now, consider whether the way you're currently operating in your life and business is in keeping with your top values. Don't feel bad if it's not—it's quite common. In fact, it's likely why you've been struggling to get into the kind of flow and alignment you know is possible for you.

STOP PUSHING SHIT
UP A HILL

So ... what would be different if every move you made was chosen from your values, not your wants? What if you prioritized freedom over followers, alignment over accolades, and being true to yourself over chasing the money?

Let's face it: things work best for all of us when we believe they will, when we want to do them, and when it feels right to do them. When we feel that lightness, that "Yes!" in our bodies. When we're doing them for their own sake, purely for the joy of it.

Guess what? Those things that feel oh-so-good and expansive in the moment will *always* be aligned with your top core values.

When you feel like, "I probably shouldn't be doing this," you probably should. Because you know what *doesn't* work? Doing things because you feel like you "should." If it feels like a big old sigh comes over you at the thought of doing the thing, *don't do the thing*. Slumping and grinding and grumping about it won't get you the results you want. It's contractive, and contradictory. Instead, check your values, and ask, "What can I do to have more ____ today?"

Sometimes, I manage to overrule myself on this. Like, "I can do it. It won't be so bad. Watch me slay this thing I can't stand." Sometimes, I almost manage to convince myself I'm having fun. But when I finally arrive, having pushed shit up a hill for what feels like an age, the results are mediocre at best. And, when I look back, I see that what I thought was the path was actually not at all aligned with who I am and what I value.

It's funny, isn't it, how deeply we already know these truths, and yet we repeatedly try to convince ourselves that we *should*—that if we just *would*, we'd get to where we want to go. That we can just "get over it."

Can I tell you something?

You never need to get over jack shit. You never need to get on with anything.

And yet, there's always work to be done.

We need to overcome our own avoidance. We need to kick resistance in the teeth and get our lazy asses up and doing what we know we came here to do.

But as soul creators, we know the difference between that work and the Stepford hustle. We *always* fucking know. You can cajole and convince yourself, bribe and threaten yourself, and you still don't want to do the damn thing, because on a deeper level you know there's a better way. A way that puts your values, not your wants, front and centre.

A flow way.

A soul way.

A *you* way which will open the *gateway* to ... well, to everything.

One hundred percent of the times I have bemoaned my lack of motivation and action-taking—*one hundred fucking percent* of the time—when I have finally stepped in and created the outcome, it came about in an entirely different way to what I was trying to make myself do.

The missing link isn't action. It's *commitment to the outcome.*

The outcome being the badass, all-in expression of your soul purpose and core values.

The outcoming being you pressing play on your life.

So, for the love of God, if you want to stand out, be seen, get ahead, make the millions ... stop worrying about your funnels, your landing pages, and your strategies. Stop worrying about the damn sales calls. None of that fucking matters if it isn't aligned with what matters *to you.*

Not once have any of my clients gotten to $50k, $100k, or bigger months because they nailed down the perfect strategy. Not once has someone said, "Wow, Kat, that adjustment to my email sequence got me seventeen new high-end clients!" I mean sure, that shit doesn't hurt. It's not *bad.* But it's not the true place success comes from. It's the cherry on top.

Here's what the sundae is:

Always, every single time, my clients created massive shifts because they figured out what mattered to them and started taking action accordingly. They honoured their souls, and decided they were unavailable

"

THE MISSING LINK ISN'T
ACTION. IT'S COMMITMENT
TO THE OUTCOME.

"

for anything less. And they went into permission for just the energy, and their fully expressed beingness, to be enough.

The same freedom, alignment, and flow is available to you.

So, get over yourself.

But also ...

Start listening to yourself.

You've always known.

You know now.

You know how.

Listen.

CHAPTER 6

YOU WERE MADE THIS WAY

I found God again while watching my children jump on a trampoline.

My daughter was bouncing away when she suddenly asked, "Why do I have to go to R.E. at school? Why can't I do Values?"

R.E. (Religious Education) was not my girl's favourite subject. Mainly because all her friends went to Values. But Values—what the non-R.E. kids did—didn't seem like the best option either. Who knew what they were teaching in that class? Probably things like "there is no right or wrong," or other insidious stuff I knew I wouldn't be comfortable with. (Or at the very least, knew I needed to understand more about.)

I may or may not have used the word "insidiously" in my response to my eight-year-old daughter. Either way, she got the message.

Then, she blurted, "But why does God even *matter*, though?"

I felt the very breath leave my body. I damn near fell on my knees in shock.

I had been run-run-running from God for most of my adult life. I was never "anti-God" or "anti-Church" or any of that. Unquestionably, I still considered myself a Christian. But actively seeking God, on the daily? Not so much.

You see, I'd gotten myself all caught up in a story that God required perfection. Like, angel-white pure perfection, all-day-every-day perfection, or else I'd be *cast down into the bowels of hell and left to burn forever!*

Certainly, I must have heard the whole "grace" bit, being as I was born in the Church and raised there for my entire young life. My grandfather and uncle were both preachers. My parents were deacons. But it never "took" for me. I always felt like I was doing it wrong. I would go to the front of the church again and again and again, but I never felt what I thought I was meant to. There was none of that sense of pure joy and lightness and unconditional love that my friends seemed to feel. And so, I gradually found myself pulling away, assigning myself the role of not-belonging, not doing it right, not being like the others.

Eventually, I gave up altogether. I just couldn't keep up. Besides, I just kept sinning—like, every time I opened my mouth. Clearly, I wasn't cut out for this stuff.

And yet, part of me always knew I'd return—and that, ultimately, I would become a leader, with a platform, asking God to use her.

Funny how things always work out precisely how we knew they would.

I, at least, was afforded a thorough education about

Christianity, and could, as an adult, make a conscious choice about how to live it—or whether to live it at all. But my kids didn't even know the basics. Sure, they'd been at Sunday School a couple of times, but they had no foundation on which to build their own thoughts about God's love, God's purpose, or God's grace. You know, all the stuff I took for granted and, deep down, still believed with all my heart?

And so, here I was, open-mouthed with shock, watching my kid jump up and down, up and down, asking me why God even mattered.

That day, a switch was flipped in me. It wasn't just about going to church again (although we haven't missed a Sunday since). I was *seeking God*.

For all of my deciding about who I was going to be and what I was going to have, for all my continual feeling of something just not being right in my life, for all the feelings of being terrified by death, for all the yammering about alignment all day on the internet when some part of me *knew* I still wasn't fully on path ...

I was ready, I decided. To know and understand and be held by God in a way that I'd never been ready for, and certainly had never allowed.

That first time back in church, I was still wondering if, this time, it would take. If I could do it right. If I was good enough for God. I was scared of judgment and hellfire. But I wasn't willing to live without God in my life any longer.

139

"

WHEN WE REALIZE THAT
WE WERE CREATED TO BE
EXACTLY WHO WE ARE CALLED
TO BE, AND FIND A WAY
TO TRUST THAT ... WELL,
THAT'S FAITH.

"

Since then, I've learned (or maybe just decided) that it's impossible to *not* be good enough for God. Feeling good enough is *what follows the discipline of being the person you know you're meant to be.*

All the stuff that stands between us and feeling good enough for God is *people-led,* not God-led. When we realize that we were created to be exactly who we are called to be, and find a way to trust that ...

Well, that's faith.

Faith, by definition, is trusting something you can't see or prove—but that you know, at your core, is true. It's trusting because you can no longer *not* trust. It's trusting because trust is the missing piece—the last bridge between where you are and where you're going.

FAITH IS THE NEXT STEP

If you've done the things I've taught you so far in this book—ditched the train to nowhere, made a decision to have what you want in the way you want it, gotten clear on what actually matters to you—you may be seeing a light at the end of the tunnel. Maybe you can even see your way clear to achieving everything you want. Hooray!

But, if you're not careful, that whole Stepfordpreneur thing can really catch up to you here. (I promise, I'll explain.)

When you decide what you want and why you want it, the immediate next step is to try to access the "how." It's logical, right?

No. In fact, as we discussed in Chapter 5, the "How" is deadly.

The "how" is the windowless room.

Some aspects of the "how" are fine. Great, even—at least, when we're talking about the rituals and practices we know are ours. When I follow my morning routine—workout, coffee, blog, journaling, get on with my damn day like a queen—I find purpose, and purpose finds me.

But that's not what I'm talking about.

I'm talking about those times when you don't have a view of the "how" from where you stand, and so you go looking for stuff to fill in the blanks. You look for systems to build that audience. You look for tactics and strategies and other people's "millionaire morning" routines. You start doing dumb shit like changing how you look to make your audience like you, filling up your time with things you hate, or shaming yourself for not being more ... whatever.

No! No! Sound the Stepfordpreneur alarm!

What if you didn't have to go looking for how to "make it happen"?

What if you just needed to have a little faith?

Recently, I've added this prayer to my morning routine: "God, use me for Your will today." And then, I let go, trust, surrender, and totally believe that whatever crazy shit I'm nudged from within myself to do will be perfectly in service to my purpose and God's will.

I trust that all my needs will be taken care of.

Fully.

Now.

Without struggle or pain.

I know that God knows what I need, and what the world needs from me. My only job is to let myself be guided down the rabbit hole and not try to figure out the whole damn thing in advance.

But if life is just one big game of trust (and it is), the question then becomes ...

Who and what have you chosen to put your trust in?

And where is that trust leading you?

If you've put your trust in other people's success, to the exclusion of your truth, you will end up robotically following their methods and madness until you crash. (I believe we've already spent enough time following that train wreck.)

If you put your trust in your own fears and excuses, you will never stray far from your comfort zone. Sometimes I oh-so-dramatically refer to that inner fear-voice as being the voice of the Devil. But it's not really that dramatic at all, is it? I mean, it's only your *life*. And if fear is in the driver's seat? Sounds like you're listening to the Devil to me. His greatest work is to take your identity and then convince you nothing happened!

But if you listen, just listen, to that pure, clear voice inside of you—the voice of God, and of your soul—and then just *do what you are fucking told,* you will find purpose.

I won't lie: writing about God used to make me want to throw up. I'm more comfortable with it now, but at first I felt instantly self-conscious, attention-seeking, vulnerable, even ashamed. *Who do you think you are?* that voice inside me says. *People don't want to hear you go on about God! What if it damages your brand? Let's talk about something less triggering ... like money!*

Ha!

But the truth is, I got where I am because I let the damn message be the message. And the message flows through me, but it comes from somewhere else.

THE VOICE THAT COMES AFTER THE FIRST VOICE IS NOT THE REAL VOICE

I ask for direction from God a *lot*. Sometimes, I don't feel like I know what I want to do, or what the next step is. Sometimes, I don't see clearly who I want to become, or where I want to go.

And so, I backslide a bit.

Yes, even now.

I'm at the point now where the things I do regularly are the things I absolutely want my life to be about. But sometimes, when I'm feeling stuck, I give myself permission *not* to do them.

When things get frustrating and hard, you just need a lay-on-the-couch-and-eat-all-the-crap-while-binge-watching-horror-movies kind of day, right?

Well ... no.

The mindless trash (food, media, and otherwise) is fun and distracting in the moment, but afterward, not so much. By the end of the day, I end up flailing, lost, and feeling kind of gross.

When you unleash the true work of your soul, sur-round yourself with *the most* badass peeps, and pretty much do whatever you're guided to do every day, the wallowing isn't fun anymore.

I know, at the end of days like this, that I would feel much better if I had just done the damn thing God had asked me to do in the first place. It wasn't that I didn't get an inner nudge. It's that I heard another, louder voice afterward, and listened to that one instead.

When you start living and taking action from faith instead of Stepfordpreneur-style prefab strategy, you will *always* hear the true voice first. It will be a whisper of inspiration, a feeling of, "Wow, that would be cool!" Then, another voice will shout, "No! That's too hard/not cool/totally wrong!" and you'll find yourself heading straight for the remote and crisps.

The voice that comes after the first voice is not the *real* voice.

Sometimes, the contrast between the first voice and the second is obvious. It's fairly clear to me at this point in my life that eating shit food and wallowing in my own indecision is not God's plan for me today, or any day. But sometimes the second voice—the not-God voice—is a lot sneakier.

Sometimes, the second voice is all about "action plans" and "meeting objectives" and "discipline." It's about following a path that worked for others because you can't clearly see (or hear) what's authentic to you.

Never once have I created an action plan, followed through diligently on every step, and because of said

"WHO AND WHAT HAVE YOU CHOSEN TO PUT YOUR TRUST IN?"

discipline "got there" in precisely the time I had decided.

And yet, here I am.

Sometimes, there's a path you can't clearly see—but God can see it. Sometimes, when I'm on the verge of a huge expansion, I see things inside me that feel right but have literally no place in my current reality—things that scare the fuck out of me. When I'm led or nudged or poked or hit with a flaming fucking arrow from my soul to say, *"Yes!"* I do it. No matter what that reasonable, practical, insidious-as-fuck second voice says.

I do them.

And then things happen.

Good things.

Amazing things. Things that bring me joy, love, and purpose.

Things that just feel good.

These things happen faster if I remember not to worry about the "how," and just follow that first voice and keep my eye on what I envision.

They happen a little slower if I decide what I'm creating is too fancy and next-level, or if I'm afraid I'm not "there" yet and start thinking I should have some sort of plan or expert advice or program. I might get caught up in this for a while, but ultimately, inevitably, I throw up my hands, proclaim, "Fuck this shit!" at the top of my lungs, and do it my way—whatever messy, random, all-over-the-place way that happens to be.

And then, it works.

YOU WERE MADE THIS WAY

It comes to life.

It becomes a part of me—so much so that I wonder how I ever questioned it at all.

Some people see this as me just being Kat. "She's confident," they say. "She's a badass. She's unstoppable. She's *somehow more pre-approved by God than me* so she gets to do what she wants, while I'm over here fumbling through and wondering if I'll ever just get to be me!"

And I think, "You have no idea!"

When you make decisions from faith—when you listen to the first voice—no one will have any idea how unsure of yourself you often are. How much you will question your right to do *anything* that isn't already "part of you."

How much you will question everything that is part of you.

How much you will worry about being "allowed" to have it all—to be blessed like that, to be taken care of like that, to be wealthy as fuck like that, to *breathe* and *walk* and *take* up space like that.

All.

The.

Time.

It's relentless, this process of kicking your own ass back to soul—of making faith-led choices and being who God put you here to be.

You will be asked to choose beyond your readiness.

You will be asked to choose beyond the "possible."

You will be asked to be who you are not yet ready to be.

You will be asked to show up where you are not "allowed."

You will be asked to exist beyond your humanness.

You will be asked to do what doesn't make sense.

You will be asked to choose what is already inside of you, without hesitation, in fullness.

And you will be asked to do it all with your feet firmly planted in God, soul, and truth, and with complete understanding that this is the only way to become who you came here to be—and who you have always been.

You were preapproved before you even set foot on this planet.

Stop wasting your time.

SOUL-LED CONSISTENCY

When I was seventeen, I looked in the gym mirror at my little baby muscles, pulled the EZ-Bar up to my chest, and said to myself, "If I keep doing this, and I'm consistent no matter what, by the time I'm forty I will be *insanely* successful, rich, and have arms like Madonna."

I turned forty a few years back. And all of what I decided has come true. (Yup, even the arms. Especially those.)

In my thirties, I used to write a little statement in my journal: "I am friends with my mentors."

During that time, I came across the writing of James Altucher. Instantly, I knew I had found a soulmate mentor. I stayed up until 3:00 a.m. every night devouring every single word of his that I could find, and grabbed any tiny pocket of time during the day, too. I was shifted and changed by what I learned from him, and was inspired to step more fully and audaciously into sharing my own truth.

Today, I'm connected to all my favourite mentors. I've met many of them in person, even though they live halfway across the world. I even got to livestream with James Altucher, my all-time favourite writer (did I mention that already?) from his New York apartment after an epic three-hour flow conversation of all things badass and soul.

All because I *decided* it was true, even before I had proof it would happen.

After reading this chapter, you may have gotten the impression that, if you allow yourself to be led by faith and soul, everything you do from this point on will be random—like, God will send you on some kind of scavenger hunt that makes no sense at first but will net you the treasure in the end.

That sounds fun (maybe), but that's not really how it works.

You can leave the "how" up to God while still being consistent in the things that are authentic and meaningful to you. In fact, you absolutely *must* be consistent about the things that feed your soul. God isn't your servant.

"IT WASN'T THAT I DIDN'T GET AN INNER NUDGE. IT'S THAT I HEARD ANOTHER, LOUDER VOICE AFTERWARD, AND LISTENED TO THAT ONE INSTEAD."

God won't magic up everything you want if you don't do your part to set the stage for the magic.

You see, consistency is how you program your body, your mind, your thoughts, and your feelings.

You program yourself to upgrade.

You program yourself to receive.

You program yourself to *become who you say you want to become.*

This isn't about pushing, making plans, making lists, and making yourself do stuff. You and I both know that shit doesn't work. But when you are consistent with what matters, you will have *more* flow. *More* ease. *More* ability to hear the messages from soul telling you what to do and where to go.

So how do you know what to be consistent with, and what to run the fuck away from?

There's only one rule:

It's supposed to feel good.

Now, when you're looking at being consistent with creating—with dancing, unleashing, ripping shreds out of your soul and sharing them with the world—you may ask, "How could this ever feel good? It's so *hard!*"

But how would it feel *not* to do it? How would it feel to let your body collapse because you feed it shit all the time and never get off the couch? How would it feel to keep your mouth shut when you want to sing from the depths of your soul? How would it feel to walk by your mentor on the street because you're too scared to

153

introduce yourself—and live the rest of your life know-ing you missed the chance? How would it feel to keep everything you want to say locked away inside you until you die? How would *that* feel?

Easy doesn't equal good.

And hard doesn't equal hurt.

So, bleed.

Sweat.

Strive.

Burn.

Go out on a limb.

Face the things that scare you.

Chomp 'em up and spit 'em out as you saunter down the street in your six-inch stilettos like the motherfuck-ing queen you are.

Ask God and your soul what you *get* to do, not what you have to do.

And do it every damn day, over and over. Consis-tently. Even when it's hard.

Because only then will you be ready to do what is *really* being asked of you.

To receive.

To be brave.

To become.

To have.

To embody.

And then hand it all over, because God has got you.

Do what you came here to do.

CHAPTER 7

PLAYING IN THE QUANTUM

I was six years into my online business, and had already made several hundreds of thousands of dollars, before I ever thought about what a "proper" sales page might look like.

I mean, I guess I kinda-sorta knew what a sales page was. It wasn't a shocking concept. I'd heard of it before. But it certainly wasn't something I thought I actually needed. Couldn't you just sell off blogs? My whole thing was about having conversations in the online space; I would listen to what people had to say, and then figure out how I could help them through the products I created. Simple, right?

Then came a point where I was ready to uplevel my online game. I started to notice that people did these extended, vaguely formulaic sales-letter-thingies, and I wondered if I should do them, too. After all, they were a lot fancier than what I had going on—which was mostly comprised of PayPal links on my—you guessed it—blog posts.

Beware the idea that the next level requires you to be fancier.

So, I hired a coach to help me become more successful in the online space. I saw the women in my coaching group doing what I was doing—but (to my mind)
they were doing it *so much better*! I was a little in awe
of them, so it made sense to me that I should emulate
them. I was a full-blown fan girl—not in a silly or needy
way, but in an absolutely committed, aspirational way.
I was determined to become the best possible student
and wring every drop of knowledge from my time with
these mentors.

So, when one of those mentors took a look at my site
and said, "Aww, Kat. It's so *cute* how you've done it" ...
well, I shrunk a little. But I took it on board. Clearly, I
had a long way to go before I reached an acceptable
level of "maturity" in business.

After that, like any good little Stepfordpreneur, I did
everything I could to de-cutify myself. I learned how to
do "proper" sales pages. I learned how to market like
the big girls. I learned how to sell in a way that fit within
the accepted paradigm of "how successful people sell."
And, as best I could, I squeezed myself into that windowless room of "the way things are meant to be done."

You know what? I learned a lot of good stuff. But the
learning came with a lot of shame. I felt like I'd gotten
away with doing things my way up until now—but if
the "real" entrepreneurs were laughing at me, calling
me "cute," and shaking their heads in woe, there was
no chance I could *keep* doing things my way. In fact, I

felt like I was being called to fix my mess before everything fell apart.

What I wasn't strong enough to recognize back then was that the only thing that really mattered in marketing was that *I was feeling it.* That it had the essence of *me* in it.

I *so* wasn't feeling this.

And guess what? It didn't fucking work.

All of those grown-up marketing tactics didn't make me more money. In fact, my income started to slide. My fancy sales pages didn't grab people like my messy, heartfelt blogs. My slick offer didn't transmit what was unfolding in my soul. I started losing ground. And no one—not me, not my coaches, not my peers—could figure out why. After all, I was doing it "right" for the first time ever.

The problem wasn't the strategies. There's nothing inherently wrong with learning how to create an effective sales page. The problem was that I thought the *only possible path to success* was to do things like the big girls. But doing it that way meant that I could no longer do what I felt called to do—what was in my soul to do.

My coaches were essentially telling me not to be me. No wonder it backfired. Especially for someone like .. well, like me. Like us.

To be fair, it wasn't their fault. They were teaching something they truly believed in. But it wasn't for me. My mistake wasn't in making the investment, or in trusting

" BEWARE THE IDEA THAT
THE NEXT LEVEL REQUIRES
YOU TO BE FANCIER. "

them, but in assuming that their way was *the only possible way* I could ever reach the goals I'd set for myself and my business. Don't get me wrong: I still got the value of the investment. It just came in a different way than expected.

Every time we fall into "shoulds," we limit the possibilities that are available to us. This is why you keep falling on your face even after you've spent thousands of dollars to learn from "the best." This is why you keep getting stuck, even after you've decided what you want. This is why, even when you try to give it up to God, you still feel sorry. Inadequate. Or worse, "cute."

In order to do it your way, you need to see possibilities for what they are: actual, tangible realities that already exist in this space and time and are waiting for you to bring them forth from your soul like the badass creator you are.

THE SUSHI TRAIN OF RECEIVING

Since you've come this far with me, it's clear that you've absorbed some radical truths.

One: that in order to start living the life you were born to live, you have to stop living the *wrong* life. Full stop.

Two: that deciding what you want is the first step to actually creating it.

Three: that once you decide what you want, the best (in fact, the only) thing to do is give it up to God and stop fucking around in the "how" part of it.

(I told you there was no "do this and that" strategy to becoming a Rebel Millionaire. It's all about being yourself, as you were created. Dropping out of the windowless room. Saying buh-bye to the "good little entrepreneur" tactics.)

But *why* does it work?

Why do you feel the truth I'm dropping in your core like a bonfire burning up your bullshit?

Why does this super-simple soul-led approach invite you into bigger and bigger expansion with every breath, every moment, every thought?

Because ... science, baby.

It's actually *not* superhuman to exist in the one percent of the one percent—to have a standard of faith and excellence beyond what most people can dream of, never mind aim for. It's not superhuman to expect and receive massive money flows simply by doing what your soul tells you to do, or to actually become the version of you that a year ago (or even twenty minutes ago) was purely aspirational.

There's nothing mystical about being the person you came here to be and, *as a direct result of that,* getting everything you could ever want showered upon you like you're fucking Cleopatra.

There's nothing magical about creating your reality exactly as you desire it to be.

This whole cosmos is one big, infinite stew of possibilities.

All of these possibilities exist simultaneously.

They're all there.

They're all available.

Have you ever been to a sushi train? You just sit there, sipping your sake, while the conveyer belt brings roll after roll, and dish after dish, your way. You choose what you want and put it on your plate. What you don't want, you leave for someone who does.

Put like that, it doesn't seem like anything to write home about. "Mum, can you believe it? There's *infinite choice* at the sushi train!"

But most people can't understand life like that. They think they have to take whatever damn thing comes down the conveyer.

And the people—like you and me—who get picky about what goes on their plates? Who refuse to settle for anything less than the flow, the joy, the millions? They tell us we're crazy. They say, "Be like us, or we'll call you weird. We'll label you as dangerous. We'll lock you away!"

Getting choosy about your possibilities isn't unnatural. Only uncommon.

Lots of people (including me, I'll admit it) throw words like "quantum" and "subjective reality" around as if they're super cool and fancy.

And they are ... but also, they're not.

They're just outside the current rules humanity has created and agreed upon. Outside the norms laid down as expectations. That's why they seem so new and "out there."

But nothing is outside God's rules.

Intuition—aka, the ability to listen to and be led by soul—is available to everyone. But it isn't commonplace, because people view it with caution and fear. Like, "Stop opening your eyes so wide! Stop seeing what I can't see! It's not normal!" Those of us who knew things, who spoke truth, who broke rules ... we learned how to blend. How to shrink. How to be accepted and "do it right."

We started taking whatever crap the sushi train dished out.

But now, we're off that train for good.

Now, we can choose.

And the choosing is just as natural, just as normal, as being able to walk, talk, and breathe.

It's also special. Amazing. Wondrous. I'm not disputing that. But is it any more wondrous than a human body that somehow navigates a three-dimensional world on two weird stalk-y things called "legs" and regulates all of its own metabolic functions without any conscious direction?

"
GETTING CHOOSY ABOUT
YOUR POSSIBILITIES
ISN'T UNNATURAL. ONLY
UNCOMMON.
"

It's scary to be a goddess warrior in a world full of stunted, warped people who have no real idea how to get what they want, or even handle life.

But let's be clear: *they* are the ones who are not normal.

The human being was designed to be all things. To access infinite knowledge from the quantum collective, and not just from the obvious. To be naturally intuitive, even psychic, and wise on a level which transcends three-dimensional learning.

We were designed to become what we always were.

So quit telling yourself that it's magic, and that giving up the "how" to God and soul is "woo-woo." Stop putting on a pedestal this idea of some "ultimate" version of you, because your idea of "superhuman" excellence, magic, wealth, and purpose? Well ...

It's the *least* of what you're supposed to be.

And it's time to accept the responsibility you've been given: to choose only the best and most delicious possibilities from the universal conveyor. Because it's *all* available.

IT'S PHYSICS, BABE

Know this: The empire you're trying to build already exists.

But because you can't see it yet—or won't *allow* yourself to see it yet—you keep trying to build on something that still feels far away. Therefore, you're perpetuating a reality in which you exist on a completely different continuum from what you desire and know is yours.

(Yes, even if you're already giving it up to God. You don't get delivery on something you haven't actually *decided*, with your whole being, to have. Nor will you easily receive on something that is not coming from a spirit-led, and *you*-led place. Alignment is everything, baby.)

What you need to do is admit that what you want already fully exists somewhere in space and time—that it's fully formed, and ready to unfold in the now, on this plane, right before your eyes.

That was what I did the first time I wrote my vision for wealth and freedom (as I shared in Chapter 4). I decided to have what I wanted—and with that decision, I made it real. With every word I wrote in my journal, I called it into being from whatever back-end corner of the universe it had been hiding in. It was already there. It just wasn't in the same version of "now" that I was choosing to see and observe around me.

The fact that you can see your rebel life—your millions, your status, your freedom—in your visions and dreams, in the musings of your journal, and in the little whispers of something that float through you and then quickly away before you can quite grasp them ... well, all those show you that your fully-expressed life is *there to be seen.* And if a thing can be seen—even if that "sight" is purely non-physical, then surely it exists. Otherwise, how would you see it?

And, if you can see it, in all its detail and intricacy and full-colour glory, but others cannot, that doesn't mean you're crazy. It means that what you're seeing is *your vision to see.* Yours and yours alone—and therefore, yours to create.

This is a logical conclusion, particularly when you understand anything about quantum physics and the realm beyond the physical.

Yup, we're about to get science-y.

Your physical body is just one aspect of who you are. You also have emotions, thoughts, your own personal electromagnetic field—a whole bunch of other "selves" that are just as powerful and important as your physical body.

What you see and feel inside of you is just as real as what you see and feel and observe outside of you. In fact, what you see inside is more real, because ... particle theory.

It's been well-proven that "reality" shifts and changes

when we're not observing it. Particles aren't particles when we're not watching; they're waves. Imagine a house full of teenagers partying away while the adults are gone, dancing like crazy, doing whatever the fuck they want (but certainly not doing what they'd be doing when their parents were around). When Mum pulls into the driveway, though, those particles instantly morph into well-behaved little goody-two-shoes who fall in line according to whatever is expected of them.

"Reality" is fluid when we're not observing it. When we turn our attention to it, it snaps into whatever form we desire and expect.

(No, I'm not making this up. Google "Double-Slit Experiment" if you want the details.)

Your reality will be whatever you expect it to be— just like wild teenagers will show their parents whatever they expect to see.

So, if you want to change your reality ...

You'd better *change your motherfucking expectations.*

Whether we're talking about a dream, a desire, a knowing of purpose, a work you are supposed to do, or simply those millions you want because money is fun, it's time to call it in. Right now. With absolute certainty and decisiveness.

Because now you know.

And even "I know I can have what I want, but I'm choosing not to" is a whole lot more powerful than, "I can't."

" IF YOU CAN SEE IT, BUT OTHERS CANNOT, THAT DOESN'T MEAN YOU'RE CRAZY. IT MEANS THAT WHAT YOU'RE SEEING IS YOUR VISION TO SEE. "

THE RUNWAY

When you're still learning how to manifest instantly by tapping quantum possibility, it can feel a lot like you're on an airport runway.

You are here.

What you want is *there.*

And there seems to be a whole bunch of baggage, detritus, and other people's planes in between you and it.

In other words, you can see the vision, but you are still perceiving obstacles in getting there.

So, let's clear the path.

Close your eyes. Pause. Tune in. And ask your soul to show you any and all obstructions to your flow—all the reasons why, despite the fact that you really want the thing and know it's divinely yours, you aren't claiming it.

(You might perceive unworthiness, cost, connections, readiness, or fear that it will be taken away, to name a few.)

Sit with this until you can clearly see what's blocking your runway. Then, make one of three choices.

One: Make your decision to have this vision so strong that it automatically wipes out all the other possibilities swirling around on the sushi train.

Two: Decide to have what you want, but with some form of cloudiness or reserve which also requires you to clear the runway piece by piece or otherwise shred the obstructions to flow.

Three: Decide that you are not actually willing to have what you want and go back to daydreaming about your millions because that's easier than actually doing the thing that will clear your runway.

Any way you choose is fine.

Any way you choose is actually simple.

Any way you choose comes with its own required action, surrender, and evolution.

Any way you choose, you're still choosing.

Clearing your runway can be easy, or it can be hard. But the only way it will be *impossible* is if you keep trying to bring something to life that you believe is still purely imaginary. You are absolutely entitled to live your whole life choosing not to choose. That possibility is floating around the sushi train, too. But I can guarantee it won't fill you up.

THE HARDEST BIT IS WALKING AWAY FROM NOT FUCK YES

If you want to put all of what you've learned here to work, at some point you're going to have to get off your sweet ass and recode at the level of practical action.

Yes, it's about playing in the metaphysical. The spiritual. The theoretical. You need to understand what's happening behind the curtain before you can actually drive this bus.

But if you had even a fleeting thought that it's enough to just *talk* about the quantum, the energetic, the dance between the physical and the ethereal, and not actually *do* the damn thing of *becoming* the damn thing ...

That's not how it works.

It starts in your mind, for sure. You have to *understand* it. You have to *envision* it. You have to *decide* it and know why you want it.

But if, after all that, you somehow came to the conclusion that you can just *think* your way into millionaire status, *feel* your way into successful, or *imagine* your way into purpose, you're in for a huge wake-up call.

Nah, babe. When you fully understand, when you actually fucking *get it* in every pore and cell and bone in your body ...

That's where the work begins.

And the truth is, it's going to *burn.*

It's going to pull you.

Stretch you.

Sear you.

And you'll be grateful for that shit, because how the fuck do you expect to become the new you without tearing apart the old?

Oh, but it's supposed to be flow! Ease! Fun! Butterflies and unicorns and *for the love of God where are the damn marshmallows?*

I mean, really. Did you think you can get to ease and flow without clearing that runway?

Did you expect to grow without stretching, moving, and *growing your damn wings?*

Yes, it *is* ease and fun and flow to call a whole new, fully upgraded, totally badass version of you into being *because you desire it.* But once you do that, you actually have to start being her. Owning her. Putting the torch to every fucking thing in your reality that is *not* her. It means doing *whatever it takes*, no matter what it takes, until it takes.

That's what it means to be one of the chosen ones.

To choose yourself.

To choose to have it all.

And the hardest bit isn't even the "doing what it takes." It's not the sweating and bleeding and crying. It's not the overcoming and triumphing and getting

"

SO, IF YOU WANT TO CHANGE YOUR REALITY ... YOU'D BETTER CHANGE YOUR MOTHERFUCKING EXPECTATIONS.

"

stronger. That part feels *good,* even when it hurts, because you know it's moving you forward.

No, the hardest bit is walking away from all the things that you're giving your life for that you know damn well are *not your actual thing.*

It's burning bridges.

It's tearing down old homes, old loves, and old habits.

It's walking into the abyss.

It's making space—and then waiting and living in that space while you stay the course and refuse to give up until the actual thing you've chosen appears.

It's diligently, ruthlessly, and repeatedly shredding *all the things* that aren't a full-on "Fuck, yes!"

Want to be a Rebel Millionaire? Make this a rule for how you live. How you love. How you do. And how you *are.*

Because otherwise, you stay stuck. You remain in the *not* fuck yes. In the "Maybe it will get better." In the "Maybe this *is* my dream life, but I just can't see it yet." In the "Maybe I am the problem and I just need to adjust/heal myself/be more worthy."

Blah, blah, blah.

If you were to simply insist on the "Fuck, yes!" then everything would change.

It's how you clear the runway.

IT'S EITHER FULLY
FOR YOU … OR IT'S NOT

When I was a teenager, my mother gave me a piece of advice that has never left me.

Even when she said it, I knew it was important. Profound. And *right*.

She said, "Katrina, whatever you do, *do not* get into a relationship with a man who is less intelligent than you. You need somebody who is more intelligent than you, and who challenges you."

I also knew, somehow, that I would not listen. That I would let fear rule me, for decades that felt like lifetimes. That I would forget so I could *remember*.

For most of my life, all of my relationships, romantic or otherwise, were tainted by the knowledge that, when push came to shove, I was the leader, and I was the more intelligent one (at least, in the way I believed intelligence needed to be expressed in this situation).

Maybe I thought it was impossible to find someone who could keep up with me.

Maybe I secretly (okay, not-so-secretly) felt like I wasn't good enough to hang with someone who was my equal.

Maybe God had lessons to teach me through the choices I made.

Maybe I let my fear of being alone dominate the conversation.

Maybe ... all of the above.

But eventually, you reach a point where you've had enough of your own bullshit. And you become willing to step into the abyss.

I did this in business. In states of total uncertainty, I hired soulmate staff members and gently let go those who weren't up to the task. I called in soulmate clients even though I knew that working magic with them would challenge me in every way.

I did it in my lifestyle by refusing to be "under command" of anything or anyone except God and my soul. This includes everything from food choices to releasing addictions to my location-free lifestyle to my strong, healthy physical body.

I did it with stuff, by refusing to be "practical" when it came to things like homes, or cars, or clothing. I buy what appears in my life because it's aligned with me. And once it's mine, it feels normal and natural for me to have it—even though it felt like a stretch before I acquired it.

And, eventually, after a whole lot of heartbreak and many fuckups, I'm learning to do it in love.

Drawing the line on what is and is not acceptable is scary as fuck. You have to be willing to hang out in the void—a place where everything you're used to doing and being and living is just ... gone.

It's not fun. It's not flow.

It's tempting to run away, settle, compromise, and let go of the vision for the "Fuck, yes!" It's tempting to do what feels easy in the moment rather than what will *be* good in the long run. That's what my mother was trying to tell me.

So, when the time comes ...

Don't do that shit.

Don't settle. Don't compromise. Don't give up.

Be *honest* with yourself.

Decide to stay in the void for as long as it takes. Whatever it takes. Until it takes.

And when you commit fully, walk away fully, give it up to God and soul fully, and fully fucking *mean it*—

That's when the magic happens.

You may have noticed that we've come full circle to where we began this conversation in Chapter 1. Makes sense, right?

Getting off the crazy train to nowhere is all about choosing the "Fuck, yes!"

Recognizing that you don't need permission is all about your "Fuck, yes!"

Ditching the Stepfordpreneurial tactics and copycat strategies is all about your "Fuck, yes!"

Deciding what the fuck you actually want (and why) is all about your "Fuck, yes!"

Deciding to give it up to God and listen to your soul is all about the "Fuck, yes!"

And leaning into the mechanics of the quantum is all about the "Fuck, yes!"

Basically, it's simple. You already know what you want. Who you are. Why you came here. Now it's time to fucking *choose it*, once and for all.

From here, we move *as if* you've chosen. As if every word you've read on these pages is seared into your soul. As if your "Fuck, yes!" is clear as a bell and you're committed to picking nothing but the absolute most aligned, delicious options from that cosmic sushi train. As if you have already brought your wildest desires into full form and are ready to start living them.

Are you ready? Let's go.

CHAPTER 8

YOU ARE THE NICHE

A year or so ago, I booked an impromptu trip to Melbourne for myself and my sister, Jessica.

Jessica had been doing some work with me in the business, and (as happens when you work with people, even if they're family), we had some stuff to work out between us. It felt kind of heavy, and I was *so* not available for that. I'm not available for any kind of rift with my sister, no matter how minor it is.

So, I decided to do something cool for us. After clearing it with her husband (since he'd need to be around for their kids), I booked us a two-day getaway at a luxe hotel so we could have some fun and just drop in together.

This was a great trip on multiple levels. I got quality time with my sis, plus time to just take care of *me*. We did a little shopping, had an amazing lunch, and then ... things started getting silly.

Maybe it was the different environment. Maybe it was hanging with Jess, who is a person I can always be fully myself with. Maybe it was just that kind of day.

But that's not the point.

The point is what happened after.

You see, leading up to this trip, I was in the middle of a launch that was—well, we'll call it lacklustre. My brother, Ash, who's my COO, told me just before we left, "This offer is fun, but it's not magnetic. Registrations are low. I think it's time to shift something up. You know this."

"Oh," I shrugged. "Well. It's fine. It will work out."

I left it at that. I knew something would shift. I just didn't know, at the time, what it would look like.

I wrote some powerful blogs over those few days away. I felt myself slipping into a flow state and rallying to gear up the energy inside myself.

Then, on Monday morning, I did a livestream from the hotel bed with my sister where we got up to all sorts of shenanigans. I was being totally immature and ridiculous, to the point where the silliness was out of control. I may have put my purse around my neck and hung a shoe from it. (What? It was a rose-gold Valentino shoe, and a brand-new Dior purse! People needed to be able to see them properly!)

I posted that livestream with a thumbnail that looked like me about to impart the fucking meaning of life ... with that shoe in hand, of course.

Despite my immature behaviour and nonsensical jokes, the message was deep and powerful—a call for people to be who they came here to be and own their uniqueness. I felt that energy transmission in every cell of my body.

The insanity didn't stop there. By Monday evening,

I (ahem) *suggested* that my sister steal a bowl of olives from the restaurant at dinner. Like, the actual bowl that the olives were in. We posted the whole escapade to my Instagram stories. (In case you're wondering, there were *very* valid reasons why we needed to take the tiny olive bowl, and it was absolutely in integrity to do so!)

The next morning, I felt totally self-conscious. Like, "Oh, God, I've gone too far this time!" I had a killer vulnerability hangover, and felt just *"ugh"* about the way I'd acted. Instead of avoiding it though, I rewatched the whole thing while on the treadmill and ended up cracking up at myself like a weirdo in the middle of the gym, because here's the reality ...

Despite my (apparent) insanity, I knew part of the reason that registrations for my launch were trickling in (rather than flooding) was that I hadn't given any real incentive for people to join early. Ash was right: what I'd put out there so far hadn't been magnetic—not in the way my best content usually is. The reality is, my products sell well when I am "in it" with the offer, not because of bonuses or extras. I need to ask myself: "Is this true for me right now? Am I in it right now? Am I in relationship with this thing I'm creating, and responding to its needs?"

In this case, the answer had been "no." The connection wasn't there, which meant the magnetism wasn't there. And therefore, unsurprisingly, the sales weren't there!

However, less than two days after my Instagram antics, I had enrolled over a hundred people into my

" WHEN PEOPLE SAY YES TO WORKING WITH YOU, IT'S BECAUSE THEIR SOUL IS SAYING YES TO YOURS. "

program. All from one silly-ass livestream and a story about swiping an olive bowl.

"I couldn't scroll past that shot of you with the shoe!" one of my students told me.

By being fully me—totally, full-on, no filter *me*—I was magnetic. I created my own pathway from soul, and it opened doors of flow. (On a not-so-sidenote, it also was a gateway to me tapping into my true power and truth—and, ultimately, the message within me that will shake the world.)

No, you don't always have to do random, funny, or nonsensical things to create flow—unless doing so is a natural by-product of you being *you*, in which case ... yeah, you probably *do* need to do those things, at least part of the time. But the *whole* time, you need to be, and let through, whatever is true.

In other words, the magic is in *you just being you*. Yes, *all* of you—even the immature, silly bits!

Maybe especially those.

The truth is, those crazy, random, all-over-the-place livestreams—the ones I call "Kat Shenanigans"—were once something I dropped into daily. They aren't part of my day-to-day now, but when I was first coming into my voice they were a big part of how I let go and let my magic flow. And whenever I do that, even now, money comes in. Soulmate peeps show up. The world is right again.

Because, think about it: How could the world *ever* be right without you being all of you?

NICHE, OR CALLING?

Truth time.

Your niche isn't your ideal client.

It's not your expertise.

It's not your mode of service.

It's *you.*

You are the niche.

You are the motherfucking niche!

You've probably read this whole book thinking, "Okay, Kat, I get it. I need to be me. But *how* do I leverage being me in my business? What's the formula? What's the three-part system? How can I sell 'being me'? *How do I do it?*"

The answer is, you do it *like you do it.*

Not like I do it. Not like that famous coach with her million followers does it.

You do it like *you.*

You can't separate business and money from any other aspects of your life. Well, I mean, you could *try*. You could sit here all day and ask, "How do I cram this multifaceted brilliance of who I am into a neat, pretty package that's acceptable to the people I've defined as my ideal clients ..."

Nah.

You could also get out your journal and ruminate on questions like, "What is the message I'm meant to share

YOU ARE THE NICHE

with the world today?" or "What am I being guided to create and put out there, and how can I adapt and position it to the brand I've created?" This would likely be a massive step up from how you're currently doing it—and how most of the world is doing it. It would have some level of impact. But if you took a big step back and looked at that in relationship to who you are, and the Rebel Millionaire life you have *absolutely fucking decided* to create, that would still feel grossly out of alignment. Why? Because this isn't about taking little pieces of you and weaving them together into some sort of pretty picture.

If you're still trying to make it all fit, you're not getting it.

The way you become magnetic in your business—the way you sell whatever fucking thing you've decided you want to sell—is to create your own pathway from what is inside you, with everything that's inside of you. It's going to be messy—especially at first. It's going to be random (although, not really). It might involve you belly-dancing on a beach in black lipstick, serenading your peeps from your bathtub, or hanging a rose-gold Valentino shoe around your neck. But any and all of those only apply if that is what your soul is screaming at you to do.

When people say yes to working with you, it's because their soul is saying yes to yours. Some blog, some livestream, some podcast, some TikTok video you did shot them straight in the soul like an arrow, and they couldn't resist you any longer. You got yourself in a totally high-vibe state and allowed your gifts to flow from you and into the people who were ready to receive them.

Of course, not every piece of content you create is going to be *that* level of magnetic. You can still create good content that helps people even when the soul magnetism isn't at one hundred percent. That's called being a professional. (Remember we talked about consistency? Creating content is one of the things I do consistently, not just because it helps me grow my audience, but because that super-flow state gets easier and easier to access when you *practice*.)

But while doing the work every day is absolutely essential, doing the work while not giving yourself permission to be all in with every fibre of your soul's calling is counterproductive—*even if it still results in sales.*

That right there is the difference between a Stepfordpreneur and a Rebel Millionaire. Is it soul-led, or soulless? Are you a creator or a content mill? Are you coming from raw, juicy, give-it-everything-you've-got fucking *truth*, or are you giving them what you think they want to hear?

There is no middle ground. There's alignment, and then there's everything else.

I missed this boat for a long, long time. I held myself back and tried to polish my image because I didn't think I was cool enough, accomplished enough, or *whatever* enough to hang with the cool kids.

I felt as though it were a true, certified fact that if I wanted to be well known in my industry and get masses of people to buy from me, then I had to change pretty much everything about me.

I had insecurities about my message. I mean, would people really want to hear me ramble on and on about living purposefully, pressing play on life, and finding flow? (The answer, of course, is yes!)

I had insecurities about my look. I just wasn't as pretty and polished as those fembot-preneurs who were *known* and successful. It was like they had some kind of code or secret superfood that allowed them to always be sleek, shiny, and dressed stunningly. Me, I'm mostly a gym chick. I have nice nails now, and a ginormous closet full of designer bags, shoes, and clothes that I pretty much only wear on photo shoot days—but I never really felt like I had my shit together image-wise. Everything about me was just so ... homemade, you know?

Maybe you feel that way, too. Like, deep down, you know you were born for more, and you're *obviously* going to do whatever it takes to get there, but there is just *so fucking much wrong about you* that you have to fix first.

Guess what? My homemade, messy, unpolished fab-ulousness has made me tens of millions of dollars. And yours will do the same for you—if you're willing to all-out own it. Because your business, life, and absolute soulmate clients *want you as you.*

Your people will love you when you start being you. Not at first. Not all of them. But the ones you are meant to impact, lead, and blow the lid off life with? *They* will love you. And they are the only ones who count.

You can change your image if it's soul-aligned and you desire to do so. But stop lying to yourself and saying that shit matters. Unapologetically own your so-called mess. There's nothing wrong with you. There's just never been anyone like you who does what you do, because, I'll say it again ...

You are the fucking niche.

No one is going to come along and pave the way for you. If you don't claim what's yours, *now*, it will never fucking happen.

Let me ask you ...

If you had nothing right now—no business (not even an idea for a business), no plan or desire to market to one carefully-curated group of people, and no one knew who you were—but you still had all of the knowledge you've gained around your topic and every other area of life—

Would you still have something to say?

I'm guessing the answer is yes.

In my experience, there are two kinds of people in the online space: those who have a deep calling and a burning message that they absolutely need to get out, and those who want to make money online and have chosen the field or path of expertise that seems most likely to create that result.

"
THERE IS NO MIDDLE GROUND. THERE'S ALIGNMENT, AND THEN THERE'S EVERYTHING ELSE.
"

For someone in the latter group, pretty much everything I've shared in this book would make no sense. They're looking for info on how-to-do, not how-to-be. It's very unlikely to resonate (unless they're secretly sick of the Stepfordpreneur game and are ready to move into soul-led work).

So, since you're here, I'm assuming you belong to the first group.

Which brings me to this:

If I were to follow you for a week and take in *everything* you do and say online—if I were to watch the way you answer when someone asks what you do; check out your website, your offers, and how you communicate; dive into what you sell and how you present—would I see a leader? A revolutionary? A motherfucking queen with something to say who is actually, clearly, publicly *saying it*?

Or would I see another "teacher"—a passer-on of information selling a way to do things and positioning herself as an expert among experts, a coach amongst coaches, another consultant with some unique spin on her ability to Teach You Some Stuff?

What if you had nobody to impress?

What if you'd never even heard of "niching" or "ideal client avatars" or "sales funnels"?

What if all you needed to do was show up every day and share something based on your life and what rings true in your soul?

Not because doing so will get you five new clients.

Not because you need to make X number of dollars this month to keep up with your mastermind buddies.

Not because some program told you that teaching like a teacher's teacher is the Key to All Success.

Not because you had to ...

But because you *could*.

You will never create true wealth from a place of misalignment. You might have money, but you'll never have true impact, or true joy in your soul-driven work.

Sure, you might make some money in the short term. You might even think, "I have to do it this other way for now, but one day I'll get there and then I'll release my True Work!"

No, you won't.

Because once you've dug yourself a niche, it's awfully hard to climb out again.

So, start asking yourself:

If you got off the wrong train ....

If you stopped asking for permission ...

If you just fucking decided to have what you want ...

If you gave up all the details (including the business mechanicals) to God ...

What would you be giving your life to, and for?

What would be exploding from inside you?

And whatever that answer is, for you, in this now moment ...

That's not a niche.

That's a *calling*.

Answer it.

LESSONS OF BADASSERY

Someone asked me the other day, "What are the lessons that truly helped you become a badass online?"

It's a valid question. And most of the answers I gave, we've touched on at some point in this book. But in case you need a refresher, let me summarize for you again.

#1: WRITE YOUR OWN REALITY

Everything I have—my boss beachside house, my luxury European cars, my killer shoe collection, my first-class travel, the fact I can spend time how and when I like with my loved ones every day, and what underpins all of this, my ability to literally show up as me every day and get paid like a mofo for it—I created first in my mind, and on the pages of my journal.

You get what you expect. You get what you focus on. And if you write it down, you'll be able to expect it, and focus on it, more powerfully.

Write it as though it's already done. Use "I AM" statements. Like, "I am super rich. My programs sell out every time I launch. I change people's lives with my message every single day." Keep writing, and keep believing.

Close to every morning—I'd say 360 out of 365 days a year—I journal. It may only be for a minute or two at times (hey, kids, biz, life!), but I take the time to go in and dream of all the things I want to see in my life, and how I want to see myself, believe, and feel about myself, too. All from a place of choosing to believe. And seeing it as done. Then, I go about my day as though it's true—because I have decided it's true, therefore it's true. Write it real.

2: BE DISCIPLINED LIKE A MOTHERFUCKER

Do the shit that matters. Do it every day.

Say no to everything that's not a full "Fuck, yes!" In other words, don't do things that aren't aligned with the results you wrote about in Tip #1.

Keep your eye on the ball. Make decisions based on outcomes, not emotions or obstacles.

Make no excuses, and tell no lies. Especially to yourself.

3: BE RELENTLESS

Eventually, you get sick of learning the same lessons over and over again. When you know you are born for more, the question isn't "Can I make it happen?" but

"Do I believe I will make it happen?"

Make your dreams non-negotiable. And be relentless as fuck in pursuit of it. Do whatever it takes, for as long as it takes, until it takes … and then keep going.

4: UPLEVEL BEFORE YOU'RE READY

Normal is defined by what you're used to.

If you want *more* and *better*—if you want to *be a fucking VIP* and have that reality be automatic—the only solution is to expand your view of what is "normal."

There's no point in staying at a five-star hotel or flying first class or investing in something truly luxurious if it's going to be a rare, almost-too-good-to-be-true thing. The only way to have that stuff be part of your everyday life is to make it your new normal.

Love good wine? Continue to see this as your norm. Take action (and browse menus) as guided. Be with expanding possibility, and act from that place!

Believe you can truly have soulmate clients? Define it. Get clear. Clearer still. Step into the vision as though it's a physical place you get to go. It is.

Dream of being a VIP and having life itself step up for you in all areas? Practice making the moves that that version of you would make. Allow your new reality to meet you where you step. It always will!

Follow what you actually wish it all could be—

because it *can.* Your desires are *the blueprint provided by your soul.*

Remember, all the things you want are already possible and already exist in time and space. They may not be in the places you are used to looking—but that doesn't mean they aren't available. It's not your job to justify what you want, or work up to it, or plan for it to happen someday. It's your job to *choose* it, and then refuse to accept anything less.

5: REMOVE THE LINES BETWEEN BUSINESS AND LIFE

The last time someone asked me about work-life balance, I almost spit out my shiraz.

Fuck balance.

Yeah, I said it.

I have no lines between my business and my life. I'd livestream from the fucking shower if it wasn't so socially inappropriate. I never feel the need to hide, to hold back, to compartmentalize. My mission is my calling is my life—and my calling is monetized because I listen to God and my soul and do what I'm fucking told.

That doesn't mean I have no downtime. That doesn't mean I have no privacy. That doesn't mean I don't showcase different aspects of myself when I'm snuggled up with a book versus posing in designer digs for a high-profile photo shoot. It doesn't mean my business infuses itself into my family life, or into *anything* I don't want it, in that moment, to be part of. It just means that I don't *for one second* think it's appropriate or helpful or safer to separate who I am in my work from who I am when I'm not working. I let it all naturally mesh together. I trust myself to be with what is. I remind myself that that level of trust is a choice! Whatever I'm doing is whatever I'm doing, and it's fully based on how I feel and what I have decided I want the outcome to be.

I don't have a lot of boundaries in business. I'm easy to access; my private clients can message me pretty much 24/7. That doesn't mean I *respond* 24/7. It just means that, again, I don't overthink it.

Get your energetic ducks in a row. Know you're *only* attracting the right people, and that your energy is the boundary! For me, I've created my entire business—from private client work through every part of my groups and even my free community—as a place I want to be, and that I am in trust with. I simply don't have people come into my space who abuse my boundaries.

Who needs balance when you have flow?

6: PUT FIRST THINGS FIRST

To be honest, this has been my toughest lesson so far.

Most days, I feel the pull of a hundred different things. I run multiple companies. I have employees, partners, clients. But I also know my priorities: go to the gym, journal, write my daily messages, show up to serve and sell in my business, do my daily money practice. After that, it's basically whatever feels like a "Fuck, yes!"

I've put off, half-assed, or totally ignored marketing and content calendars. I don't bother to edit or clean up my blogs before I hit "publish." I've diligently written my task list at night and then just as diligently ignored it the next day and proceeded to instead do whatever the fuck I wanted. All because none of these things were "first things," nor were they "Fuck, yes!" things.

I know what moves the needle in my business and my life. Everything else is a distraction. If I'm not *extremely fucking disciplined* around what matters, I won't get the same results.

7: REMOVE "MAYBE," "HOW," "CAN'T," AND "WAAHHH!"

You don't have time for that shit. Seriously.

You are not a victim ... unless you choose to be.

Let that sink in.

Begin to be in the practice of being in the practice of being the person you know it's time to be. (Yeah, the repetition was deliberate. Know what else is? The place you choose to act from.)

8: SELL UNAPOLOGETICALLY ALL DAMN DAY, AS A BY-PRODUCT OF YOU EXISTING.

When you remember that *you are the mofo niche* and start being your whole badass self in your work, selling will feel so much more natural. You'll be *so excited* by what you've got on offer that you will just talk about it. Over and over. It will never get old.

I do it like this: Create unparalleled amounts of free value by virtue of being me and sharing my truth. This gives me permission to offer to help people take the next big leap. I mean, it would be selfish of me not to make an offer at that point. After all, if my work is speaking to you and you *know* you need to level up your fucking mindset and action, why *wouldn't* you want to know what I can do to help you get rich, famous, and successful? And if for some reason you prefer to fight your own fight and not say yes to money and truth right now, God knows I've got enough free content to keep you going for years.

9: BECOME THE LEADER OF YOUR OWN REVOLUTION

Shout your mission from the rooftops.

Choose confidence and self-belief.

Call forth from your soul a message that moves millions.

Lead the way with your words, your actions, your look, your body, your relationships, your whole damn *life.*

When all is said and done, leadership is what makes a leader. So, rip off that Band-Aid and start acting like there was never any choice but for you to jumpstart this thing. Now. Today.

Remember, it's all there already on the quantum sushi train. It's been created. You just have to step the fuck up, make it your new normal, and refuse to be, do, or accept anything less.

QUIT THE OVERTHINKING.
LET IT JUST COME OUT!

The reality—which may make you squirm—is that, when you step into your unapologetic truth and fully-expressed beingness, you kinda sorta abso-fucking-lutely can just "make shit up as you go," and it will *work* because God and your soul know that you're on purpose.

And, at the same time, you're not making up anything, actually. You're allowing through the product of who you've chosen to be for years now. Why would you hold that back?! Why would you edit or filter it? What a crime!

You have to understand this—

When you stop making your "Fuck, yes!" wrong, you will allow more flow. More soul. More money. True Rebel Millionaire money! But best of all? The absolute certainty you are being who you came here to be. Doing what you came here to do.

And it is *good*.

As for all the stuff you ignore in favour of doing what you soul is screaming at you to do?

Let God sort it out. You might choose to add an occasional "get shit done" hour where you intentionally do just that—but you don't need to keep living from a place of trying to be on top of things, be enough, or be anything other than *you*, unleashed.

In fact, doing anything other than unleashing all of you would be destructive to your every dream.

Because I listened to soul, I became one of the most consistent and prolific content creators on the internet and gained a soulmate audience who buys my shit on repeat without ever caring about the details.

They're not buying my courses.

They're not buying my coaching, my VIP days, or my expertise.

They're buying the energy and fuck yes of me just being *me*.

This is not for everyone. It's not for the faint-hearted. But for some of us … it's the only way it was ever meant to be.

So, what are you waiting for? It's time to *say yes* to being all of you. Again, and again, and again. And then *throw it at the world.*

CHAPTER 9

THE MONEY SWTICH, BITCH

have a tattoo that's particularly important to me. It gives me a buzz of satisfaction and a deep "Yes!" every time I see it, or even think about it. It's on an angle sloping across my ribs on my right side, and it says, in my own handwriting: *When I say yes to soul, life says yes to me.*

I got this after spending the month of January, 2018 in Bali. Enzo had asked to take the kids for several weeks over the Australian summer break. So, I decided to head to Bali—which, if you have a month of time to spend solo, is a pretty ideal spot. For a whole month, I would have nothing at all on the schedule except a few sessions with Vlad, my amazing tattoo artist.

For my home base, I chose a luxury villa at a lesser-known luxury resort which I adore for the privacy it provides. The views, food, and amenities are exceptional as well. I would have total solitude and high-end service, plus a twenty-four-hour personal butler on call (which I *love*). My villa was in Seminyak, a part of the island that I know well. Hidden from the tourist areas and crowds, all the things I desired and needed—read: gym, hot yoga, the best food and wine—would still be within walking distance.

I don't know if it was just the magic and headiness of Bali—which is certainly a thing, and one of the reasons I find myself there so frequently—or something else, but within minutes of my arrival, something massive shifted inside me.

I walked out of the airport and into the thick, soupy air of the energy vortex we call Bali, and I felt it pass through me. I felt myself become one with the power *beyond* me. My body became floaty. The hard edges of my mind softened. The needing to know, or do, or even really *care* about anything fell away.

I was home, home, home. *Soul* home.

Then, things got real.

If you've ever been to Bali, you'll know what I'm on about here. Those first few days when you arrive (or return), it's not uncommon to experience something I like to call "being Bali fucked."

No, not fucked in a good way.

Fucked in the *best* way—in a weeping and cursing and gnashing of teeth way, with a whole lot of shit coming out of you in every possible way.

Bali will detox anything less than soul truth right out of you, if you allow it and are open for it. (And, sometimes, even if you're not.)

During this period of being Bali fucked, anything

"THERE IS A SUPERHUMAN SWITCH INSIDE OF ALL OF US. WE CAN GO TURBO AT ANY TIME. WE ONLY NEED TO STOP RELYING ON THE DOING AND THE PHYSICAL WORLD TO GET WHAT WE WANT."

and everything that can go wrong, will. You may become physically sick. Your tech will do whatever the fuck it wants, but definitely not what *you* want. You may simply feel so energetically spent that you can barely move.

Me? It was all of the above. I spent entire days lying naked in the foetal position on the deck of my villa. (Which makes for an awesome tan situation, by the way. *Not!*)

We all need shit to be stirred up in our lives some-times. We need to be brought to our knees in order to let go of all the ridiculous stuff we've told ourselves about who we are and who we are not. We need to be brought back to soul.

It was exactly what I needed. And what I had chosen.

When you come through this sort of energetic tumble dryer, having shed all the shit you've allowed to build up inside of you, having dropped your guard, having let go of anything not in this now moment, having been weakened and humbled, you come to a place where you have *no choice* but to rely on your magic. The veil is lifted, and you just know—

What is truth.

What matters.

And who you *are.*

Suddenly, you're dancing and floating and flying with life itself, at one and in sync with the heartbeat and pulse of the universe. The steps are shown to you right when you need them, and not a moment before. And you're fly, fly, flying so high you can barely keep up.

Magic switch, *flicked.*

Catch me if you can, baby!

There is a superhuman switch inside of all of us. We can go turbo at any time. We only need to stop relying on the doing and the physical world to get what we want.

In fact, when we try to do it all ourselves, we are often brought to a point of what seems like crumbling, but which really only exists to force us to remember that it's not all on us. That we have to let go of the "how." That we have access to magic, collective energy and knowledge—and, of course, God and soul.

Dramatics aside, that's what Bali did for me on that trip, and so many besides. But really, was it Bali? Or was it my full surrender? What do *you* know it's time to let go of, and allow? Remember, you can't sow new seeds without clearing the debris from last season's field.

That first week in Bali, the letting go, the "you can no longer ignore this" truth of my soul, was so absolute, so deep, and so all-consuming, that it's no wonder it ended up being my biggest sales week in my business to date.

Once I could lever myself off the deck again, it was as though I couldn't put a foot wrong. Moment by moment—but only right as the moment came upon me—I knew exactly what to do and how to do it. More, it felt like what I was being shown was so random, so left field, so *not* something I could or would have ever thought of on my own, that I just had to trust and do it.

I did upward of $325,000 cash received in sales that week.

I onboarded several brand-new, very high-level soul-mate clients.

I dropped all my extra body fat in a matter of days. I looked like I'd just done a twelve-week body transformation.

I barely slept, but I had insane, superhuman energy.

And, most of all, I had a deep and complete sense of certainty that I was in the right place, doing exactly what I was meant to do, in exactly the way I was meant to do it. I was being the highest, fullest expression of me, whatever it looked like in that moment.

Call it "dialled in." Call it super-flow. Call it going quantum. Call it whatever the fuck you want.

I call it being exactly where I was meant to be, and being fully present.

(When was the last time you did this? Allowed this? Became this?)

As I gazed into the mirror in my villa one day, feeling wonder and awe at just how rapidly reality could change when I just fucking *allowed* it, it occurred to me that all of this magic was actually very simple.

In every possible way, from the smallest detail (such as what fruit I chose to eat for breakfast) to the biggest (what next move to make in my business), I was *saying yes to soul.*

214

And, as a result of that?

Life was saying yes to me.

The veil had been lifted, the mask dropped, the curtain pulled back. All of a sudden, I saw what I had never been able to fully see before.

The answers are always, and *only*, within.

It's not about what you do. It's about who you are. Action in a particular area does not automatically equate to results.

And nowhere is that more evident than around money.

IT'S TIME TO
LISTEN TO SOUL

None of the concepts I just explored were new to me when the plane landed that week.

Since you've read this far, they aren't new to you, either. And yet, here we are.

You've probably been waiting since the moment you picked up this book for me to reveal the Big Secret to Making Millions.

Well, I just did.

The Big Secret is *fully operating from soul alignment.* I define this as observing, admitting, and then *owning* what is in you—followed by acting accordingly, from that place and *only* that place.

Before January of 2018, I'd been actively creating my business around "soul certainty" for a long time. But, that week, something deeper opened up. A new abyss of trust opened at my feet, and I fell into it, because I had no choice. (Shitting myself on a deck for days, remember?)

And from that point on, my business revenue exploded.

Later, I had my revelation inked on my side, so I could never forget: "When you say yes to soul, life says yes to you."

The reason we've come this far together in a book titled *Rebel Millionaire* without really talking about money is this: you will *never* attract the kind of money flow you desire, in the way you desire it, until you surrender to soul flow.

This is why all the courses and coaching and formulas and tactics haven't made you the millions you dream of: you haven't come to a place where you fully trust that life will give you what you want. You still think you have to force it into being. Like if you just clean every corner of your windowless room and arrange your desk and hair just so, eventually you'll find a giant pile of cash.

No!

What you want can only be accessed from the beyond. From the quantum. From the supernatural. From God, and soul, and the spiritual "Fuck, yes!" of being who you know you came here to be.

From *being all of you*, and saying yes to all of you, so life can say yes to you.

It cannot, and will not, happen from a place of non-trust.

Oh, and also ...

- Sort-of trust = non-trust.

- Almost trust = non-trust.

- Conditional trust = non-trust.

And honestly, knowing that soul and the universe want nothing more than to say yes to you, and give you everything you desire—knowing that God made you exactly as you are, with the full intention and expectation that you would show up fully and *honour the fuck out of that*—why would you offer anything *less* than trust?

I know you're tired of waiting. I know you're damn sick of it. And trust is scary, especially when you don't already have a fat stack of cash in your wallet to prove that it works.

But what you want *cannot occur* when you push, pull, breathe, do, and create from non-trust.

And even if you're particularly hard-headed, stubborn, and relentless, and you do manage to rustle up some millions, you will never reach the heights you are destined for until you surrender to God and soul.

"**YOU WILL NEVER ATTRACT THE KIND OF MONEY FLOW YOU DESIRE, IN THE WAY YOU DESIRE IT, UNTIL YOU SURRENDER TO SOUL FLOW.**"

You will burn out. Feel purposeless. Start to hate your fucking life. I've seen it over and over again.

But, you already know this.

Your work isn't to follow a strategy and create a gazillion spreadsheets to map your way to millions. It's to do what I've already taught you: map your outcomes daily; decide to have what you want *right now*, thank you very much; and then surrender, hand it over, and get into the damn vibe of being you.

I've worked with clients who have all-out resisted this. They hired me thinking they would get The Big Money Secret. In the words of one of my private clients a few years back to our Inner Circle coaching group: "I'm sure, like me, you all wanted to reach through the computer screen and punch Kat at first." Sometimes, we need to keep hearing the shit that drives us mad—and *I will keep saying it until you finally, fully learn the lesson.* Just like I did (and continue to do) for my highest-level private clients.

That guy who wanted to punch me? He now makes *millions* every year from his soul-led work. The rest of that Inner Circle group is doing the same. You can also do the same.

Just stop making it so motherfucking complicated.

DECIDE THAT IT IS NO LONGER A PROBLEM

I'm sure I'll catch hell for this one.

This isn't about privilege. This isn't about "worrying about money is a choice for me because I make millions every year and my life is awesome."

This is true no matter who you are, where you are, or what's in your bank account. Yes, obviously, privilege exists. However, you always have the starting point of being fully you, and choosing from there how to springboard away from or deeper into that. Do you get it?

It's not about comparing you to me, or you to anyone, for the purposes of who has more or less, or what is far and unfair. It's about comparing who you are letting yourself be right now to *who you know you are*, and asking yourself what you want to do with that.

Remember when I shared in Chapter 4 about that period in my life where I was over $100,000 in debt? (Let's be honest: at points, it was pushing $150,000.) At that time, my brother, Ash—now known as the amazing COO of Katrina Ruth Companies—was working as an accountant in a firm in our hometown of Melbourne. He was also *my* accountant, and the only person with a real, behind-the-scenes look at the financial shit show that was my company at the time. He knew that my life revolved around me running on empty with my back against the wall, having to pull rabbits out of hats daily to keep afloat. I had no clue how to surrender or how to receive, let alone grow a massive abundance of wealth.

During this time, I developed a nasty habit of ignoring Ash's calls. Truthfully, I avoided him like the plague.

Why? Because I knew he was calling to see what I planned to do about my ever-increasing tax debt. "Perhaps," I could practically hear him asking, "you might one day like to ... pay some?"

A novel idea.

The truth was, I had no idea what to say to him. I kept setting goals to get the money, and money definitely showed up—sometimes even in large sums—but somehow there was never any money to pay my taxes. No plan I made seemed to work for me. So, what was the point of me answering the phone?

And then, one day, I read something which spoke to me in a way that nothing else on this topic had, ever. It was relevant to any topic where you have no idea what to do; when a problem seems so big, so insurmountable, and so real, that you can't seem to see beyond it.

This writing spoke to the depths of my soul. The piece was about 10,000 words long, but the crux of it reminded me ...

I instantly knew what to do. It was so fucking clear, so fucking simple, and such a fucking weight off my shoulders. Finally, the plan had appeared! Praise the Lord!

I picked up the phone and called Ash.

"Let's talk about my taxes," I said.

"Have you finally come to your senses and put a payment plan in place?" he asked.

"No, I have another solution."

"Good, because this is stressing you out. I mean, it's even stressing *me* out. And the worse it gets, the harder it will be to extricate yourself. So, what's the plan?"

I paused dramatically and took a deep breath.

"I have decided," I said slowly, "That it is no longer going to be a problem. I've decided that I'm just going to ignore it and focus on what I'm meant to be doing instead. I have decided it will just ... go away."

Ash was silent for a moment. (When he tells this story, he says that what he was thinking but didn't express aloud was, "She's finally lost it! She is *actually* certifiable!")

From the outside, it must have seemed that way. Inside, though, I felt clear and certain for the first time in forever.

That was my first step into actually discerning how I work with money, and how money works with me.

I literally went on to do what I said I would. I decided that it was no longer a problem, and that it would sort

"IT DOESN'T MATTER HOW YOU DELIVER IT. IT DOESN'T MATTER HOW YOU FORMAT IT. IT DOESN'T MATTER HOW YOU SELL IT. IN THE END, ALL THAT MATTERS IS THAT YOU SELL IT, AND FOLLOW WHAT'S ALWAYS BEEN INSIDE OF YOU."

itself out *because I fucking said so*, so there! I mean, I'd already spent endless time trying, futilely, to figure out the "how," analyse the "why," and shift my beliefs, and it hadn't worked. This approach was really the only option left. I mean, I sure as fuck wasn't going to give up and get a *job*.

Now, let me be clear. What I decided *wasn't* that my tax bills were going to magically disappear. I knew they would get paid. I just didn't know how—and I refused to waste any more time trying to micromanage that process.

Instead, I put my focus on my soul work. My genius work. My purpose. My message. Me.

So, what's the punchline?

Well, that shit got paid.

How?

I have no fucking idea. Neither does Ash, really. It just sorted itself out at some point over the next year or so, exactly as I'd decided it would. Sure, in a literal sense, moves were made. I could write a whole book (and might, someday soon) about the daily ins and outs of money flow and receiving. But the real revelation here was the energy shift, and the power of my decision and my *yes*.

Today, Ash loves to tell this story at our live retreats as an example of how everything—even taxes—can work out when we just decide what is going to happen and leave the "how" to God and soul.

ENTRY LABEL

THIS FORM MUST BE INCLUDED INSIDE THE FRONT COVER OF EACH BOOK YOU SUBMIT, therefore cut it from here and duplicate it as often as necessary. Insert the label inside the front cover of each book submitted (if you enter one book in one category, you must insert this form into each of the four books sent).

FOR AUDIOBOOKS: please send 3 Audible gift codes to Terry Nathan at terry@ibpa-online.org. If your book is not available on Audible, please contact Terry Nathan for additional options.

5 - Business and Career
CATEGORY (NO. AND NAME)

Rebel Millionaire
TITLE

Marie SaoBento
CONTACT PERSON

WorldChangers Media
PUBLISHER

41 Johnson Road
CONTACT PERSON'S ADDRESS

Foster RI 02885
CONTACT PERSON'S CITY, STATE, ZIP

401-252-6078
CONTACT PERSON'S TELEPHONE

marie-saobento@worldchangers.media
CONTACT PERSON'S EMAIL

https://www.worldchangers.media/
WEBSITE ADDRESS

Please indicate the book's target audience:

Women entrepreneurs, aged 20-40 who want to create

authentic personal brands

So often we think that our decision, our holding the vision, our giving it up to God, applies to *everything but money*—as if money is somehow totally separate from everything else in the universe, and plays by different rules that only a select few understand.

Nah.

If you're still thinking that way, it's because you haven't decided—fully, unequivocally decided, with your whole body and soul—that money will no longer be a problem for you.

I mean, you *could* spend the next decade or more going back and forth and round in circles trying to figure out a formula that doesn't involve *you just fucking deciding.* You could work on your commitment issues, your leadership issues, your self-worth issues, your comparison-itis, your lack of organization, your website, your social media, or your offer stack ...

Or, you could just go straight to the end goal.

Say it with me now.

"I have decided that money is no longer a problem for me."

Now, straighten your shoulders, do your best hair toss, and go get your fabulous Rebel Millionaire life.

THE BACK END

So many people have asked me over the years, "Kat, can you show us your back end—you know, where the money gets made? Where people pay you on repeat because you set up some fancy, automated shit? Where you made things all fancy and exciting and pro-fess-ion-al?"

Should I tell you what my back end *actually* is? Or shall we continue with the illusion of some fabulous money-making formula?

Your back end, front end, middle end, any old end, is whatever you put in place to facilitate an experience for people that moves them (emotionally), inspires them (spiritually), and excites them (energetically)— and then inspires them to take action (physically).

That's it.

The truth is, you know exactly what will move them, inspire them, excite them, and spur them to action. Because that's the art pouring out of your heart and soul every day.

I've said it before, but we'll go there again:

People don't buy your products, your projects, your formulas, or your services. They buy *you.*

Your energy.

Your vibe.

Your truth.

Your art.

Sure, I have systems. Processes. Things that look nice. All of this came from me simply showing up and being the person I knew I needed to be that day. None of it was worked out, built, or figured out. It all came straight from the chaos.

If you want to make sales, give them what they want, which is all of the above. Emotionally, spiritually, energetically, physically—all of it. However it comes out. From trust. And from being all of you. It doesn't matter how you deliver it. It doesn't matter how you format it. It doesn't matter how you sell it. In the end, all that matters is that you sell it, and follow what's always been inside of you. Because when you be all of you, people—specifically, *your* people—can't look away.

It doesn't matter what the "grown-ups" in your industry are doing. It doesn't matter what they've "proven," or tested, or engineered. It doesn't matter how they get people to join their email lists, buy the first shit they sell to them, upsell them to the next shit, and so on and so forth.

And yet, you think that once you have this "foolproof" system in your own back end (which, as we know, is where the magic millions come from!) you will suddenly be able to la-de-dah your way around the internet, doing whatever you please every day while you get paid.

Every single time I have put the back end first—every single time I spent thousands of dollars to build out systems and strategies and automations so I could make money on autopilot like the gurus promised—it was wasted. Totally, one hundred percent wasted. Like, I-had-to-tear-that-shit-down-and-start-over wasted.

Because what got me here—and what will get you there—was never a magic bullet. It was never taking my eye off the ball of being fully me in order to go do something I thought I should. Which is really my point here. It was whatever random truth, madness, mayhem and brilliance I let forth that day to move people, inspire them, excite them, and spur them to action.

The art is the motherfucking strategy.

You do you. You create your art. Your art touches people's souls. They follow you. Then, they buy your shit because you make a practice of *selling through your art* every day.

So, if there is any remaining confusion about how this all works, let me lay it out once more (because you know I will slap you with these truths until they sink into your skin):

You decide to have what you want.

You say yes to soul.

You give it up to God.

You keep being you. But all of you.

You take action *only* based on what is genuinely shown to you as an action to take, a move to make, and *choose* to trust that you will know and hear what those actions are.

You back this trust up by acting on it even when you're not ready.

And you do it over and over, whatever it takes, for as long as it takes, until it takes, and then you *keep doing that shit because it's the whole reason you came here.*

SEPARATE THE MONEY FROM THE ART

I don't want to let you go without saying this:

If you want to get paid for doing what you love, don't demand that doing what you love will pay you.

Trying to make your art make money for you will kill your muse dead and ensure that what you put into the world is little more than a weak, transparent dribble.

When your game is to monetize your soul work, and you've not yet learned how to do that *without trying* to monetize your soul work, everything you create will make you sick—and also keep you broke, or at least treading water.

So, what gives? Isn't this whole game about alignment, and monetizing your message and art? Isn't that the *whole fucking point*?

Well, yes.

But also, nah.

"NEVER LET THE SELL SHAPE THE ART."

To get to the point where I am—working "only from soul," just being me, throwing my art at the wall to see what sticks, and also making a lot of money and impacting a lot of people—I had to separate my art from the sell.

Before you get all riled up, let me explain, because it's actually quite simple.

If you follow me on social media or read my blog, you may have noticed that I write whatever is in my head that day. No filters. No structure. Sometimes not even proper punctuation. I let my art flow. Then, I create a separate piece of sales copy at the bottom of each of my posts/blogs/rants to let people know about the next big thing I'm doing. Often, there's a line or a heading or some other divider between them.

The point is, *I never let the sell shape the art.* The writing comes from my soul. The sell comes after. They are two separate things.

Every single artist I have known or observed who is in their genius zone and doing their soul's work *and* is also monetarily successful has done the same thing. The only way you will get paid for being you is to stop trying to craft your art for consumption. Don't put conditions on your art. Don't ask it to jump through hoops to create predictable outcomes. Don't ask it to lead to something. Just let it show you what it came here to do.

And when you get that high-as-a kite, fully expanded feeling that can only come from saying or writing or giving life to whatever is coming through you? Your soulmate clients will find you.

If you can't pronounce that you are willing and now choose to do what you are really meant to do, for the rest of your days, the way it was meant to be done—with no filter, no editing, no trying to "make it something"—even if you never make a dime ...

If you can't do that, you don't understand purpose or destiny at all.

WANT TO RECEIVE MORE, FASTER? SURRENDER

You know all about this one by now.

Can you surrender too many times? *Never. There is no such thing.*

When is a good time to let go, lean into faith, and give it up to God? *Always.*

When should you hold your hand up to your own self like a stop sign and refuse to make a damn move until you surrender? *Every. Single. Time.*

So, pick your damn socks up. Shoulders back. Boobs out. Decide the mindset, beliefs, energy, and action you want to have around money. Decide that money is everywhere, available as air, and available for *you*. Decide it gets to be simple because you said so—

And then, do the most rebellious, out-of-control thing you could possibly do with your life, your art, and your millions:

Give it up to God.

And keep showing up.

CHAPTER 10

THE REBEL LIFE

The first week I met my Lisa, she told me all about how she intended to turn her one-woman house-keeping business into a million-dollar professional cleaning company (plus, you know, a few other businesses on the side). Of course, I hired her to clean my house on the spot.

Since then, in addition to keeping my house gorgeous, she has continued to be exactly what a Rebel Millionaire is—someone who moves forward relentlessly in the direction of her vision by listening to soul. And as of the time of this writing, she's building her soulmate team to help her cross that million-dollar mark.

She's doing this despite the squirmy discomfort of letting go of even more control.

She's doing this whether or not it's easy.

She's doing this whether or not she feels ready.

I couldn't be more excited for her.

Most people I meet talk about wanting to be millionaires and build successful businesses. But do you know how many people actually create that? Hardly any.

How many of them *could have* created this, and still could? All of them.

Here's what it comes down to—and what I said to Lisa just a few moments ago in my kitchen as I made my coffee before heading upstairs to write.

"It's so ridiculous that most people wait for the vision to come and tap them on the shoulder and tell them exactly how to do it. That isn't how it works. You must step in if you want to create it. You can't wait until you think you've gotten to it. You *go to it,* and then you go beyond it."

Life will step up to the standard you set. To the level you expect.

So, if you expect to have to *do* that process of *working toward* where you want to *one day* be ... that's what you'll get. The work. The waiting. The "maybe someday."

You've learned a lot in this book. Some of it is conscious, through the words I've spread across these pages. Some of it is energetic—a vibration that is now buzzing in your soul and your bones to whatever degree you've chosen to allow. What may have seemed impossible—becoming a millionaire on your own terms, doing your soul work—you now know is possible. This book is proof.

Now, it's time to take it one step further, and start seeing your life as a Rebel Millionaire as normal and expected ... because *of course* it would fucking look like that.

I see it as normal—and really, just the most basic standard to ask for or expect—that my company makes hundreds of thousands of dollars each month, consistently, with no deviation. I see it as normal that all I need to do is exactly what I'm guided to do, day by day, and that the entire thing revolves around me being all of me. I see it as normal that there is no part of me which it is not entirely appropriate to be, and in fact that the more "me" I am, the more everything grows, and flows, and goes. The systems and structures my family, my company, and my clients require are born not from any existing Stepfordpreneurial model, but from me *la-di-dah*-ing all over the place and listening to soul.

I see it as normal that I have a soulmate team—all of whom can read my mind and do what I want, often before I even know I want it. They can operate sans management like a well-oiled machine to get my message out even more, in an even better way for the greater good of all of us and the planet.

I see it as normal that I remain in exceptional shape and youthful vibrance regardless of my age.

I see it as normal—as my basic, expected standard—that I get to buy anything I decide or choose, while also tithing and giving and saving and growing a range of investments.

Most of all, I see it as normal that all of the above just happens as an outcome of me doing the only job which is my job to do: listen to God and soul, say

"Fuck, no!" to every possible "should," and just submit to the message and the art, over and over and over again. To do my work not for the sake of outcomes (because those are expected and normal and in total alignment), but because it's my work to do while I'm here on this crazy planet.

Did I work my ass off to get here? Yes. I would say I work harder, and "do" more in the average day than nearly any person I know. Try and stop me. I was born this way. It's nothing to do with "what is required," and everything to do with who I want to be, and always was.

But I would also say that I do jack shit except mosey around all day, following the flow of the day and the nudges I receive from God, and doing *only* what I want.

As a Rebel Millionaire, you get to go to bed every night knowing that you are in integrity and fully showing up for your life, in exactly the ways God and your soul intended. Knowing you are inspiring, impacting, and serving others, to the level that you *must*. Knowing that your "have it all" life is natural, easy, and normal—

And that you deserve every last motherfucking bit of it.

CONTINUOUS UPLEVELING

Maybe right now, or in the time it took for you to read this book, you've already noticed an upleveling. When you're in real alignment, shit happens *fast*!

You're going to love your new reality. You're going to walk around like, "I'm a Rebel Millionaire, bitch! Look at meeeee!"

But eventually, there will come a day when you can no longer muster up the energy and excitement you had before. This will affect your ability to snap new opportunities into being, sign up perfect soulmate clients, reach your next fitness or weight goal, or expand your bank balance beyond the level of your (already amazing) new normal.

When this happens (and it will), I want you to know …

It's your job to shift that shit as fast as you can, because stagnant energy is your soul's way of telling you, "It's time to go bigger and call in *more*!"

Then, being the go-getter Rebel Millionaire you are—the kind of badass who *knows* she gets to choose her outcomes—who *knows* that money and all other flow vibes are always available—you'll try to deal with the stagnancy by working harder, digging deeper, and making more of a concerted effort to strive for what you want.

When this happens, remember—

You got this far by being who you are and following your soul, even when it scared you. Even when you had no idea how. Even when you "knew" you couldn't—and then, somehow, you *did.*

Maybe you were so sick of being bound to a life that didn't serve you that you eventually just found the way out and jumped. Maybe the fear and soul exhaustion simply became greater than the "what if." Or maybe it was just because you knew it was always what you were meant to do.

At some point, you've already made a leap like this. Maybe not this big, or this scary, or this audacious—but you have been here before.

The struggle and uncertainty will always be there— at least a little bit. This life you're making for yourself is so great, it feels scary to step up and choose *more.*

The stepping up will always be there, too. It will never be done. There is always a next level, a bigger mission, a drop into *more.* Because the more you say yes to what God and your soul are offering, the more will be shown and made available to you. It's inevitable. You can't force it—but you can't fight it, either.

And honestly, why the fuck would you want to?

GOD WANTS YOU TO WIN

Imagine if, from this day forward, you made every decision from a place of knowing that:

- God made you exactly as you are, to be exactly who you came here to be.

- You have full access to every amazing bit of what this world has to offer.

- Life itself was built for you to win.

You now know that all of the above are possible. I mean, if I've done it, you sure as shit can too. That's the whole reason we're here.

Now, all that's left is for you to go forth, and *do* the damn thing of *becoming* the damn thing you desire most in the world.

Being a Rebel Millionaire is, in essence, being so fucking radical that you are willing to live out these truths at the highest level, every single day, no matter what. (Which should not be radical at all, but what are you gonna do?) And, being a Rebel Millionaire is being so *soul certain* that you refuse to accept what other people classify as "real" and "inevitable." Being willing to do everything you've learned and witnessed and dissected in this book, in your own unique way, according to the blueprint of who you are and who you came here to be.

That, my rebel friend, is *freedom.*

No longer will your fear and carefully overthought moves rule your every damn breath. No longer will you throw away vast chunks of your previous time as you try to cram your soul flow into someone else's "foolproof" system. No longer will you spend half your time turning round in circles, contradicting yourself, and refusing to claim what you desire because you can't rationalize your soul-deep *belief* in your art and soul work.

No. Fucking. Way.

Instead, you will wipe the slate clean.

Go all in at being you.

Decide.

Refuse to fuck around with fear.

Give it up to God.

Recode yourself through soul-led action, every day.

And change the fucking world—

Because you were *born for more.*

Everything you've ever needed to become who you came here to be has been inside of you the whole time. It was there before you picked up this book, and it's there now—only, now, hopefully, you can see it more clearly, because now, you have finally reclaimed the *one*, the *thing*, the *you*, and—

You've said yes to it. To you.

Meant it.

Committed today and the rest of your life to it.

And meant that, too.

Isn't that the best feeling in the world?

Repeatedly saying no to *you* makes sense, I suppose, before you see that's it's actually possible to say yes. But now you know, and *I* know ...

You will never fucking do that again.

You're awake, now.

Your soul life is waiting.

And you are *here for it.*

Life is now.

PRESS PLAY.

KAT XX

ACKNOWLEDGMENTS

My eternal gratitude and thanks to the following incredible humans for the role that they have played, and continue to play, not only in the beautiful unleashing of this book, but in the continued unleashing of me!

To Bryna, my amazing editor and publisher, who stayed a very long course with me, held the faith always, saw me for who I really am from the moment we met, and absolutely stayed in the vision that I can create the book I am here to create in a way that is fully true for me. I am deeply thankful but also humbled by how gently and calmly you held space for me as I faltered all over the place, wanting to change things a million times, before finally coming back to truth. I cannot wait for the next book with your support!

To Mim McGowan, the one woman in the world who can use my words nearly as powerfully as me, and who has done so for eight years while growing with me on my team and learning the delicate dance of crafting copy and word flow which is a yes in my soul to represent my company: thank you for everything you have done and walked through since beginning to work for me, everything you have shifted into, and the many times you have stayed through the chaos!

To Mandy Perry: I love you, sister, so deeply. Thank you for being willing and able, even in the space of me being your mentor and you my client, to call me forward when I diminished my power, and to reflect my own teachings back to me in such a perfectly articulated way.

To the entire Rebel Millionaire community, aka my online community and fam, and all who have entered into, been on, moved on from, and will still join me on, this journey: thank you for saying yes to *you*, and for seeing me in my brilliance. It is the greatest joy and honor to lead and serve!

To all my private clients, past, future, and present: you activate my truest and deepest work. The debt can never be paid!

To the man I love and adore beyond what I ever knew possible, and am in awe and wonder to get to do life alongside: thank you for being the King who was always going to be, 'of course.'

RESOURCES

For free Rebel Millionaire resources, tools, downloads, money activations, and more, visit:

www.therebelmillionairecoachinginstitute.com/bookgifts

ABOUT THE AUTHOR

Katrina Ruth is a writer, speaker, and mentor to the world's highest-performing CEOs, entrepreneurs, athletes and entertainers. Based on Australia's Gold Coast, Katrina is the founder and CEO of The Rebel Millionaire Coaching Institute, a multiple eight-figure coaching brand with nearly two decades of growth behind it and clients in over 120 countries.

Katrina's work comes back to one core truth: now is always the time to say yes to what's inside of you—and that version of you is available *now*. She is featured regularly in *Forbes, Entrepreneur, Success, Business Insider, Fast Company,* and more. She lives primarily in Australia's Gold Coast with her two children and her French Bulldog, Storm.

Learn more about Katrina's work at www.thekatrinaruthshow.com, or connect on Instagram @thekatrinaruthshow.

ABOUT THE PUBLISHER

Founded in 2021 by Bryna Haynes, WorldChangers Media is a boutique publishing company focused on "Ideas for Impact." We know that great books change lives, topple outdated paradigms, and build movements. Our commitment is to deliver superior-quality transformational nonfiction by, and for, the next generation of thought leaders.

Ready to write and publish your thought leadership book with us? Learn more at www.WorldChangers.Media.